Praises For
Rich-Minded Mom,
Poor-Minded Dad

In his new book, the author explores the influence of a child's family and environment on his development as a person.

How does parental failure affect a child's success? Why doesn't "for good" always mean "good?" How to meet the expectations of adults and not destroy your future?

The answers to these and many other questions can be found here in this fascinating book.

—Валентина Рябинина

***

On analysing the book, *Rich-Minded Mom, Poor-Minded Dad*, the author is helping parents in a humorous way to bring up children to become strong, independent and self-confident individuals who are not afraid to follow up on their dreams. It can also help anyone willing to raise one's standards, and, more importantly, wishing to take their life back on track.

—Jana Horackova

***

On reading Federico's new book, I must say that I'm looking forward to putting into practice many of the teachings the book recommends. In this regard, the author faces a difficult topic: the education of children, and how the parents' thinking and ideas can have a critical impact on their future lives as adults. A topic which, to some extent, affects each and every one of us.

—Marina Neurin

***

A great insight into how the beliefs and habits of your parents shape you as you are growing up. Full of personal anecdotes and lessons learnt through experience, Federico's book is an insightful source of tips and tricks to avoid letting people control your life. We can't change our family, but what we can change is our strategies and our outlook, and this book can help you to better your own life.

—Lucy Toms

***

The book gives you an honest opinion in the parents' behavior towards their children, and the influence the former can have on the latter, and how a parent's thinking can either encourage or discourage their sons or daughters' plans as far as their future is concerned. Besides, the book explains how we can easily be either victims or protagonists of our lives, based on the decisions we make. This is why parents, children's prime educators, must be very careful about what thoughts and ideas they decide to plant in their little ones.

—Luca Beninca

RICH-MINDED MOM POOR-MINDED DAD

A Manual About Life

Federico Siggillino

Published by KHARIS PUBLISHING, an imprint of

KHARIS MEDIA LLC.

Copyright © 2024 Federico Siggillino

ISBN-13: 978-1-63746-224-9

ISBN-10: 1-63746-224-7

Library of Congress Control Number: 2023944510

All KHARIS PUBLISHING products are available at special quantity discounts for bulk purchase for sales promotions, premiums, fund-raising, and educational needs. For details, contact:

Kharis Media LLC
Tel: 1-630-909-3405
support@kharispublishing.com

I dedicate this book to all the rich-minded parents in the world.

Keep teaching your children not to give up,

especially when things get tough.

Table of Contents

WHY I HAVE WRITTEN THIS BOOK

My previous book, *The Greatest Version of Yourself: A Journey Within* (2020), was written to make myself and you, dear reader, reflect on life. This new piece of writing is centred on family, my family.

I am again focusing on life, but this time from my parents' perspectives on a number of life's matters as far as teen upbringing is concerned. Being accustomed to writing with an open heart, I have no trouble admitting that I was influenced by *Rich Dad, Poor Dad*, by Robert Kiyosaki in the choice of the topic. However, despite having taken the idea from Kiyosaki's bestseller, my book and his feature a few differences. *Rich Dad, Poor Dad* talks about finance. Mine deals with life in general. The former is focused on Kiyosaki's real dad (the poor dad), and his friend's father (the rich dad), whereas my own work focuses on my biological parents, despite using fictional names throughout. Kiyosaki's writing primarily focuses on picking up key financial lessons to become financially free. By contrast, this book is about life's everyday vicissitudes – what one should do (or not do) when making important decisions.

Based on perspectives, know-how, and common sense, I will talk about the rich and poor suggestions my parents gave me during my years as a teenager. That said, it goes without saying that this piece of work is not only unique, but also original. Biographical, yes, but not boring. In fact, its purpose is to be thought-provoking, to make the reader ponder life, ways parents can lift their children up, but also ways to take them down if they are not careful.

Why take them down? As you read, I will explain this, but for now, I anticipate that from personal experience, many parents have a limited perspective on life. Very limited, indeed. All too many parents have never really pushed themselves out of their comfort zones, nor have they ever questioned their own beliefs and ideas. Neither have they gone against everyone's will to follow one's heart, nor have they taken on any real challenges or risks, such as leaving one's country and friends to start over somewhere else.

Personally, I have lived abroad for many years (and still do). This changed my life completely in terms of thinking, manners, and values. I have learned to take care of myself in all aspects of life. And there is more to it. It allowed me to question my "Italian" ways, ideas and beliefs I grew up with to that point. What I did was put the above to the side, and I picked up new ways, ideas and beliefs along the way. I made a blend of different backgrounds and settings, creating a new, more enriching world for myself. This is essentially how I became a more organized and proactive person over the years — a better version of myself, if you will. This is something that I could have never achieved by simply living in my hometown.

During my time away, I've learned, for instance, to be flexibly minded and to see things from multiple perspectives, to see that there is, for example, more than one way to achieve a goal. On the contrary (and I noticed this many times), those who didn't travel other than for sightseeing or typical tourism were more likely to only consider their own points of view and wanted to be right all the time. This is what I call being delusional, and living in a "small world." As such, it is difficult to make such people see your point (however different it may be), or ask them to change their minds, as it is essentially their way or nothing. That is, I had to either step down, or an argument was likely to follow.

This is when I realized how astounding the differences can be between those who travelled (again, not as tourists), versus those who didn't. This is also when I noticed the importance of questioning one's beliefs and ways and making a habit of challenging oneself on a continuous basis.

Unfortunately, individuals stuck in their small worlds can also include those most dear to us, like our close friends or parents. Having lived too long in the same villages or towns, they have adopted a so-called small way of thinking. For the record, I also come from a village, so I know what it means to live too long within a close community and to stagnate as a result. The only difference is that I was lucky enough to have someone in my family to push me to get out of my bubble, turning me into the open-minded person I am now.

Despite the fact that living in small communities can be pleasant for countless reasons, it has its downsides, too. In fact, spending an entire lifetime in the same environment, surrounded by the same people, is likely to shrink your mind rather than expand it. It mistakenly brings you to believe that there is just one way of doing things, one unique method to figure things out. I would argue that this is not intentional, but rather a side-effect of too much sameness. Over time, having never experienced something different, these same people naively think that what they know is and must be the best way forward. We know that this is delusional, but ask yourself: how many times have you seen your colleagues, friends, or acquaintances stuck in their own ways? Was that perhaps because they were taught by their own parents, or had always worked in one unique workplace?

The problem is that when we adopt a tunnel-vision approach, we limit ourselves a lot; we are preventing ourselves from really coming out of our shells and seeing life as it can be – *an infinite source of abundance and joy*. The primary reason why many people lead a miserable existence is because they don't see this abundance, despite it having always been there for the taking, waiting for anyone brave enough to see it and, more importantly, embrace it.

When you are told that you must study, work your entire life, and then retire, that's tunnel vision. When you are reminded that you must go to university in order to find a good job, again that's a limiting belief. And when you are told you must either study or work (implying no room for anything else), that's yet another shrinking approach.

I am stating all of this because this is exactly what I was told non-stop by my dad during my teenage years and first years as an adult. How wrong he was in advising me about life's greatest decisions. Just because he was taught by his parents (that is, my grandparents) to live in a certain way, he wanted me to go through life in the same way he did. Now, my parents have always seen things very differently from one another, in terms of friendships, relationships, work, and school, but also children's upbringing. Not surprisingly, they got divorced in the end. The differences between them being too numerous, that was the only way out.

I have entitled this book *Rich-Minded Mom, Poor-Minded Dad: A Manual for Life* for three reasons:

First, to bring up all of my parents' differences when it came to my life and career choices. As individuals, we are all different from one another. Unfortunately, the same goes for parents. They may have different opinions and points of view, but when their child's future is at stake, it is paramount that they take care in what they teach their child. Second, I want to demonstrate how puzzling it can be to follow one parent and deliberately ignore the other when divergent opinions are in place. And finally, I wish to point out when disobedience is necessary, especially when it can make a huge difference for the future... *your future.*

With life not being a PlayStation® game, there is no "reset" button to press at will. Once our best years (and youth) are gone, they are gone. All too often, many teenagers and young adults listen to the wrong parent, and then regret it many years after. This is why we need to be extra careful when we come to a crossroads and need to decide what to do with the best years of our lives. Notably, our parents play a critical role in the choices we make. Since we live under the same roof as them, they are in close contact on a constant basis. As such, they can heavily influence our decisions, opinions, views, perspectives, anything – be it education, work, or love. They have their say in pretty much anything we say, do, and think. This is how they can easily cause us to detour towards their way of thinking, be it enriching or not.

If you are at an age when important decisions are yet to be made, I hope this book can be of great inspiration to you. The following pages will show you how. As you read, you will learn when to listen to one parent, and when to ignore the other; when to treasure their advice, and when you should not; and finally, when their perspective is worth listening to, versus when you should disregard their old-school thinking, and follow your *Path* – the one *The Lord* meant for you.

INTRODUCTION

When you possess great treasures within you,
and try to tell others of them, seldom are you believed.
—Paulo Coelho, Brazilian lyricist and novelist

People usually see what they want to see. Too focused on what is before them, they often disregard the abundance and prosperity available to them.

Our world would be a much happier place if only we widened our views and horizons a bit more. By simply adopting a wider perspective, we would be less miserable and smile more. After all, let's be honest, how far can one go by living with a limited view? How can a person be a good parent, educator, or guardian if they don't open up their own mind first?

Parenting is one of the most rewarding jobs in the world, but also one of the toughest. It requires non-stop dedication and commitment. If we partake in sports, we know upfront how hard we need to work if we want to achieve results, and that we must be dedicated and disciplined, but that also means paying the price of training in all weather conditions. Now, it is way easier to play when it is warm and sunny, but try to train early in the morning, in the middle of the winter. Would it still be fun? Doubtfully so. Unfortunately, parenting is similar. It is not an activity you can perform only when you are in the mood. It takes non-stop dedication and commitment on all occasions, regardless of time, mood, and weather. This makes it hard, but also very fulfilling, if done properly.

This book goes through the parental process, taking my parents and myself as an example. I aim to show how boys and girls can get easily detoured by parents' advice on their way to adulthood.

Speaking of the latter, parents usually do their best to give their sons and daughters all they need: food, accommodation, love, and so on. Some even go the extra mile by covering them up with toys and all sorts of gifts. What's wrong with that? Nothing. After all, what a parent wants is to show their affection and how much they care. There is only one big BUT, as martial artist Bruce Lee is credited for saying, "Instead of buying your children all the things you never had, you should teach them all the things you were never taught. Material wears out, but knowledge stays."

Parents are the first teachers in a child's upbringing. Especially during adolescence, children need support, valuable advice, and direction. This span of time (age 13-19) is particularly hard for them, as they are transforming, becoming men and women for the first time. In fact, it is very common to feel lost during these years (I felt lost myself back then), as it is the time when one needs to decide what to do and become for the rest of their lives.

Despite parents doing their best to assist their boys and girls throughout these messy years, there is something they don't teach, or perhaps many don't teach it the right way: *attitude*. Now, most dictionaries define "attitude" as "a settled way of thinking or feeling about something." So, why am I saying attitude is not taught, or if it is, it is not often done in the best of ways?

It's true that most parents do all they can to provide what is needed to ensure their child's well-being (food, clothing, shelter, love, you name it) and to make their path as smooth as possible, but what they frequently disregard is character. Or, to be more precise, a winning one. That is, how to behave in the face of problems, and how to react when confronted with life's most unexpected obstacles. Parents, like anyone else, may have a job they hate, or may struggle financially. They may have a messy life themselves and feel overwhelmed in many ways. As the majority of parents struggle in the face of life's most common matters, finding it difficult to be happy themselves, how can they possibly transmit a winning mindset to their children?

Personally, rather than covering them up with presents, as the Bruce Lee quote states above, I believe that what parents should do is teach their little ones to stand up for their dreams, to do all it takes to give objectives a tangible form. More importantly, parents should persist in this teaching, even when it seems most uncomfortable, and procrastination kicks in. This means not just seeing what's around them, and accepting the first given opportunity (like taking any available job, for example), but to fight for something they believe in; to bug people (of all statuses), to have their say, and show their personality. How often have we missed golden opportunities because of this? Because we were afraid, lacked confidence, or simply thought we were not ready or skilled enough?

Rich-Minded Mom, Poor-Minded Dad goes through this by taking my personal experience as evidence. On bringing up several events, you will see one parent adopting a winning attitude, the other, a poor one. I describe my experience of having one teaching me to do what I liked and to follow my dreams (whatever they stood for), and the other always suggesting playing it safe and accepting the first given opportunity, no matter what.

The differences between my parents are essentially these: one was uplifting, tenacious, and wanted their child to reach new heights. The other was pretty discouraging, with a negative view about life. One would make decisions focusing on courage. The other would compromise out of fear and low self-confidence. And lastly, one would reason in terms of abundance, the other in terms of scarcity, settling for less just to avoid the unforeseeable.

Sadly, numerous are the parents out there who similarly plant a poor mentality into their boys and girls. Being convinced that the world is lacking in opportunities, they forcefully convince themselves – then try to convince their children, too – that upon becoming adults, one should stop daydreaming and face reality for what it is: a place in which to survive. Simply put, this means seeing what is available, picking up something regardless of personal preferences or aspirations, and hanging up the boots. Unfortunately, picking up something from the menu of the available opportunities is rarely in line with what one expects, and not by random, the scarcity thinkers claim: "Be happy as you are," "You cannot have everything, you need to choose," or "Better this than nothing."

If you are a parent yourself and behave like this, you are unconsciously passing on the message to hang one's head and let life control you, letting events take the lead, rather than fighting for a spot in society. Oftentimes, this is what makes us so unhappy and unfulfilled. How can anyone feel satisfied when they wake up in the morning, knowing upfront that they will spend the rest of the day doing something they hate, or don't like anymore? Feeling stuck in a position they would love to quit, but cannot, due to financial reasons?

In teaching children to be professionally, economically, and socially content as they are, you indirectly block them from really blooming into winners in the future. You are influencing them to be stuck, and stay stuck forever, in their little boxes.

As you will see in the following chapters, the same happened to me. My dad did his best (again, unconsciously) to bring me down with his limiting beliefs and average mindset. This was a recurrent issue at home, and my parents, Tony and Mary (not their real names) argued a lot as far as my upbringing was concerned, which unsurprisingly led to their divorce. Given a similar scenario and parental mindsets, it's not a coincidence that most people today have a hidden talent, but are unaware of it. They have potential, but allow it to stay dormant forever. Parents need to show a degree of risk-taking to help their child discover what this talent might be.

Only by being truly tested,
will one awaken their true powers within.

Being taught to play it safe at all times is not living; it is, rather, *half-living*. In fact, there is a difference between fully living, and merely surviving, or between being happy with what's on the menu versus creating your own opportunities.

Being insecure and inexperienced, teenagers cannot always decide for themselves. This is the reason why they need full support from their families. Even more so, if you are a parent at the moment of reading this, or are planning to become one soon, rather than being like many modern parents, you should thoughtfully consider pushing your little ones to take on challenges as often as possible. Modern parents often tend to be over-protective, over-caring, over-everything. Teach them to be fighters, not victims in society. Pass on the idea that they can choose for themselves, rather than let someone else decide for them. It goes without saying that good times tend to pamper us. It doesn't take a genius to realize that overly comfortable times create weak, lazy people. On the contrary, hard times forge strong characters:

Everyone likes the easy stuff,
however, not everyone likes to sweat.

As stated in the previous pages, the aim of this writing is to be thought-provoking, to make readers reflect on themselves, and to think twice before blindly obeying one's father or mother, especially if one (or both) are old-school or too limited in terms of perspective. Unquestionably, it is their right to educate, however, living your life on their terms, by their perspectives, is a different story. Since it is your life, and only your life, you and you alone are accountable for what to do and how to live. It is your choice if you want to play it safe or the opposite.

I am not stating that you should rebel anytime parents, guardians, or teachers try to advise you. Far from it. All I am suggesting is that when one or both parents seem too close-minded and behind the times, take what they say with a pinch of salt, and then make up your mind. Countless are the individuals who follow their parents' words, only to regret it later in life.

I know a guy who had a flair for drawing. Rather than turning it into a profession and becoming an artist, his parents convinced him to drop it, go straight to university, and study law. Not good enough for that field, he eventually dropped out and went to work in hospitality. Many years later, the same guy got promoted as a floor manager, doubled his income, and settled down. Is he happy? Unfortunately not. He may have a permanent contract and a good paycheck, that's true, however, his heart has never been in it. Maybe it was at first, but after so long, his mind and soul were somewhere else. Unfortunately, with a family to feed and bills to pay, he feels stuck in his position and is too scared by the prospect of quitting. He may be economically independent, but deep inside he regrets listening to his parents when he could have really chosen for himself and for his best years ahead. But the damage was done, and he felt irreversibly doomed as a result.

This is an example of how many of us end up getting steered in the wrong direction by someone's poor, or over-protective advice. Very often, we listen to one or both parents, take to heart whatever they say, and then regret it forever. Has this happened to you or someone you know? Possibly.

As for me, having parents with discordant ideas in many matters is something that puzzled me on countless occasions. Why so? Because, if one seemed to be right, the other was wrong by default. This is why I wanted to share these scenarios with you in the following chapters, not only to entertain you, but also to make you think, and to show how hard it can be to only listen to one parent, but deliberately disregard the other.

I was fortunate enough to have at least one rich-minded parent, Mary, my mother. I listened to her but, more importantly, I learned from her. I would not have achieved many of the things I have achieved if it hadn't been for her. The following pages will show many of the hardships I went through and how I concluded that to listen to only one parent, and ignore the other, was the best choice I could make. If you think I was stubborn or rebellious, so typical of teenagers, I invite you to think again. When one's future is on the line, people's advice must be taken thoughtfully. One must be selective, not only with friends, but family's teachings alike, and let in ONLY what is enriching you, discarding all the rest.

Taking all this into account, I sincerely hope you can draw some useful inspiration from *Rich-Minded Mom, Poor-Minded Dad*. I invite you to see both sides of the coin: one old-school, the other open-minded; one conservative, the other ground-breaking; and lastly, one average, the other successful. Because, let's be honest:

A good life is key to one's happiness, but it all comes down to the decisions you make.

LIMITATIONS WE THINK
WE HAVE

"If someone tells you 'you can't'
they're showing you their limits, not yours."
—Dwayne Johnson, actor

Oftentimes, we are told not to do this and not to do that because it is dangerous, complicated, or even impossible. What we don't realize, at least at first, is that what limits others does not necessarily limit us as well.

We mistakenly think that our world is also the world of others. When we hear our loved ones discussing specific issues or circumstances, being older and more experienced than we are, we wrongly believe that they are right. So when they claim something is too dangerous, complicated, or even impossible, we naively (and blindly) believe them. This is the reason why most of us don't even get started. This is why so many never make their dreams come true, let alone be consistent all the way through the process. After all, let's be honest, when something is thought to be beyond our limits, why bother?

This is often what happens when we are among friends, acquaintances, colleagues, but also family members. Very often, we share our beliefs, plans, and goals out of trust. We voice our personal matters in the hope of getting some sort of support and, why not, some valuable advice. What happens is that we get repeatedly put off by the *limiting beliefs* of others. This is how, for instance, too many parents destroy their children's ambitions from a tender age. They dismiss them by telling them things like: "Be realistic," "Stop daydreaming," and the like. Simply put, they remind us to be real. What they don't understand is:

Dreams release us from our mental chains,
giving us the opportunity
to create the most wonderful things.

Assuming that studying a particular subject, or doing a specific job, is too demanding, at least to them, parents do all they can to steer their boys and girls into other directions, perhaps to something easier and more feasible in comparison, at least in their minds. Have you ever shared your ambitions or plans for the future, and were put off, or criticized by those around you? Were you labelled as weird or not having your feet on the ground? For me, this happened a lot. For a great deal of time, I believed what my parents said, especially Tony, my poor-minded dad.

Usually, because our parents and grandparents have lived longer, we believe they're wiser. Well, while they may have lived more than us, the children, this is not always the case. Personally speaking, I can agree that the latter may have seen and lived more, but this doesn't put them in a position to advise those around them at all times, and in all subjects. If something appears to be difficult to them because they tripped over it before, this does not necessarily mean it must be difficult to anyone and everyone else, too. Let's take university as an example. Many pupils get discouraged by their families to undertake certain paths because the latter think it is too difficult, not well paid, not very promising, is too hard to complete, or may give no guarantees of finding a good job. This is how, indirectly, they teach us to fly low and play it safe.

Fortunately, not everyone gets dissuaded, nor do all parents put their teens off either. When someone is very determined, no matter what people say, he or she will go for the chosen path. By contrast, those who lack clarity or confidence (like me back in the day) are more inclined to listen to family and friends, taking to heart whatever they say. This is how many make up their minds only after receiving outside advice. And if our loved ones think something is bad for us, guess what? We take in their suggestions and take a detour in our plans and, as said above, we fly low and play it safe. Don Miguel Ruiz says in his book, *The Four Agreements,* that, "the only way to store information is by agreement."[1]

He also says that all humans are made up of agreements in terms of good and wrong, and these agreements are usually passed on to one another through opinions, ideas, and beliefs.

If in a family there is a passion for a particular sport or hobby, for example, there is a high chance the children will grow up with the same passion. Not by chance, one of my childhood friends has a father who is passionate about skiing and cycling. As an adult himself now, my friend is both a professional skier and undertakes cycling competitions, and it all started with his father, who planted his passion into his son's mind at a tender age. Unfortunately, the same holds true the other way round. My mother has always had an aversion for snails and blue cheese. Result? I grew up thinking these foods were bad and must be avoided at all costs. I could not understand why, but psychologically I linked them to something repulsive, or negative in general, all because I heard my mom talking negatively of those things non-stop. This is how, unconsciously, her *agreement*, to use Don Miguel Ruiz's words, became my agreement, too.

If we think about it, the above examples speak volumes. We tend to hate things, but not necessarily because we have tried them out first-hand, and then formed a specific opinion about them. Rather, we dislike them due to external opinions, and we then formed our own beliefs based on what others have said. On a deeper level, this happens every day all over the world through brainwashing mass media. Parents, too, influence their children's subconscious minds with their already formed *agreements*. So too do our friends and colleagues, both in good and bad ways. Children are even more impressionable and tend to believe whatever they are told. Their brains are still forming and refining and they cannot think critically. This is why they easily soak up everything they see and hear around them. By contrast, teenagers are less impressionable, but still are prone to believing their peers, or whoever they stay mostly in touch with. According to many studies, we share and accept ideas and opinions of the five people with whom we are mostly in contact. In addition, acceptance of habits and beliefs is also due to a permanent fear of getting rejected if we don't conform and be and feel part of something like a group, a club, a gang, you name it. Other times, we share ideas, values, and beliefs because we have a craving for believing in "something" at all costs. This is how, for instance, nonsensical fashions spread so easily, especially among the young. Determined to fit in, they have a deep desire to be part of something. It is not a coincidence that most smokers light up their first cigarette not because they decided to do so of their own accord, but because they were long enough in the company of smokers. To feel accepted by their peers, they copied their habit.

As we have seen, our minds are full of accepted agreements, and the younger we are, the more we are likely to accept others' agreements – both good and bad – without reservation, especially if we have a gut feeling that this or that behavior will make us feel part of something. This is why parents play a key role in their offspring's upbringing. Confused and in search of an identity, teenagers need valuable advice and recommendations from someone in whom they can place their trust. This is good, but be mindful of this:

> **If parents have a limited mindset,**
> **their children are likely**
> **to grow up with one too.**

This is how people's old-school and limiting beliefs get passed on to newer generations so easily. If you recall from above, parents can be as lovely, accommodating, and caring as anything, but then they may unconsciously teach their little ones to settle for less, to avoid risks, and live a life that is below their potential. And all of this for the sake of security.

Why are so many individuals just fine with making a living? Just making it through the month? Most likely, because they were taught this way repeatedly in the past. They were told that this is what life is all about: finding a job, getting married, having children, and then retiring with what they have put aside.

Teenaged boys and girls have hopes and dreams but get routinely suffocated by those who should encourage them instead. They are constantly reminded to be realistic, to have their feet on the ground, and that dreams don't pay the bills. This is a huge alarm bell. This is also the reason I have decided to write this book. I not only wanted to show reality as it is, but also to make people – future parents, in particular – better educators, so they would avoid the mistakes their parents probably made with them back in the day.

My poor-minded father Tony also used to tell me over and over again to find a job, any job, in order to be independent. On the contrary, my rich-minded mom preferred me to find an occupation that I liked. She didn't necessarily mean one that paid well, or had good benefits, but one that would satisfy me at my core, both professionally and personally – something definitely more precious than all the money in the world.

Unlike Tony, my mom considered personal happiness and fulfilment over anything else. After all, as she always reminded me, what is money compared to long-term satisfaction? As we are continually told, money can, indeed, make one financially independent, but once that aspect is sorted, what's next? When we wake up in the morning, grumbling, and dragging ourselves out of bed, how can finances compensate for our deep dissatisfaction?

Unfortunately, most of us behave that way, especially on Mondays. We hear the alarm, hit the snooze button, and keep on sleeping until the last available moment, a sign of resistance to what's ahead. Back in the good old days, we were so excited for Christmas and birthdays that we would even wake up before the alarm. As adults, we do the opposite. We set the alarm and hit the snooze button because we don't want to face what's ahead.

It goes without saying that we all need to work in order to earn a living, but it also is true that we should occupy our days, weeks and months doing something we enjoy. If you are one of the many who were taught to settle for less, to trade happiness for money, this would explain why you may now be so unfulfilled.

Rarely is the first option up to our "real" expectations.

According to Tony, I should have gone to work straight after school. Having dropped out of school himself long before, he never liked studying. As a lad, in his heyday, he worked both in a factory and then in the restaurant kitchens. In his view, any job was fine, as long as it provided a safe paycheck and economic independence. This was his idea of the job world, and he wanted me to reason the same way. Mary also worked in factories and restaurants when she was younger. Knowing how hard it was, she preferred me to study for as long as I deemed necessary. In doing so, the chances would be higher I'd find something I liked and studied for. She wanted it this way because her parents (my grandparents), never allowed her to follow her passion which was drawing. They chose for her and sent her to study mathematics to become an accountant instead. In their view, some subjects were more important than others. To them, subjects like drawing or painting had no particular value. Plus, my grandfather didn't consider his daughter particularly clever either. This is essentially how they chose for her. Unfortunately, since it was a forced decision, Mary never clicked with math and eventually dropped out.

Since my grandparents were opposed to my mother's passions, the least Mary wanted to do when she became a mother was to let her son choose for himself. She wanted to let me go ahead as I pleased, without forcibly imposing her will on me. Living in a tourist area like Lake Garda in Northern Italy has both advantages and disadvantages. On the one hand, there is always work for those in need of employment. On the other, the only available jobs are in hospitality, like hotels and restaurants. During high school, I was still uncertain what to do with my future life, but since I was still studying, I didn't really want to face the music, and postponed the matter for as long as possible.

As we were in a tourist area, my father wanted me to go in for a career as a receptionist or a waiter in one of the many hotels around the lake. It was a good chance for me to work and be near home; that was his perspective for me. Go through the menu, see all the available options, pick one, and cave in. By contrast, my rich-minded mom had a different view. It is true that we were lucky enough to live in a tourist hot spot, and that employment was not a problem (at least in hospitality), but it was also true that if I didn't like the available options I had already tested for myself during the summer seasons, I should create my own. That meant moving out, going to university, or abroad, and choosing from a wider menu of available options.

A big truth lies in the above lines: you can either choose from the menu of available options, or you can decide to create your own. It goes without saying that the former is easier and the latter much less. What to pick? Bear in mind that life is one opportunity and one alone. Thus, a person should never ever leave their future to chance. Mary was a clear example of this. Many years earlier, she was forced by her parents to choose what they wanted from the available options near home, only for her to give up a few years afterward due to personal dissatisfaction.

What was a limiting belief for grandparents eventually became a curse to Mary, who eventually dropped out and went straight to work without a diploma. Her initial aspirations to become a drawer, a painter, or a designer, were put to bed forever, especially after starting her own family. Her greatest satisfaction was to let her son choose which route to follow on his own – to give him the freedom she was never allowed to have. That meant not necessarily choosing from what was on hand there, but making a point of choosing from a wider menu elsewhere, if necessary.

She hoped I would believe in something and fight to achieve it. So it is not by chance Mary will be the rich-minded parent throughout the book. Listening to her opened my eyes. As we will see in the following pages, I did make choices I would have never made otherwise. Thanks to her, I learned to fight for my ideas, rather than settling for less and sheep-walking with the flock.

The flock in question were my peers and schoolmates from my hometown. They went to the same school as I did, and had the same teachers. However, upon completing their studies, the majority refused to move out due to friends, partners, or simply out of fear. This is how, despite having degrees or diplomas, they opted for choosing from the limited menu of available options, settling for less as a result. Most likely, my childhood friends and schoolmates also had parents like Tony who taught them to see what's available around them, carelessly pick one option, and hold on to it until retirement.

These are decisions that people make, and I for one respect it. The only issue is that, if taken lightly, hasty choices can become a bitter pill to swallow, and turn into big regrets later on in life. How many got married, had children too early, and then broke up a few years later? And how many bought a house and signed up for a long mortgage, and then struggled to pay for it because they lost their jobs during an economic crisis or a pandemic? And how many easily got themselves caught up in the rat race because of hasty decisions? Quite a few.

Too many people I know have regrets. They voice their concerns of being stuck due to family and bills. They too would like to travel, start out a long-overdue hobby, or take up a specific course, but they promised to do so once they quit working – that is, after retiring. As Robin Sharma says in his book, *The Monk Who Sold His Ferrari*, "Never put off happiness for the sake of achievement."[2] Meaning don't wait to be too old, or to have accumulated a small fortune to start living, because how can we really enjoy ourselves when we lack the energy, have ailments, or have voids of memory every other day?

Thanks to my rich-minded mom and her teachings, I learned how beneficial it could be to pursue the less-crowded path and that, despite being scarier and more uncertain, it is also the only one leading to personal satisfaction and enduring success.

As Thomas A. Knight reminds us, "If you try, you might fail. But if you don't try, you'll never succeed."[3]

Be a rich-minded person (and parent) yourself:

Fight for your own ideas. Do not let others' opinions detour you. Don't be afraid to go against the grain. If your peers choose one way, you do not necessarily have to join in, especially if you have a gut feeling that it is not in your best interest. Your personal satisfaction is way more important. Friends come and go; it is not the end of the world if at some point they choose to exclude you. Trust your sixth sense more often. Be selective about the people you surround yourself with. Everyone can give suggestions, both rich and poor ones. Your job is to wisely recognize those individuals who can lift you up with ever-fresh input and great ideas. Be alert on this and make a point of ignoring the masses and their perpetual limiting beliefs and poor advice. Do so, and it is guaranteed you will go far.

THE IMPORTANCE OF READING

"Reading is essential for those who
seek to rise above the ordinary."
—Emanuel James Rohn, entrepreneur

Since antiquity, human beings have always noted down their thoughts. Be it in the form of scrolls, papyruses, or letters, they have always written, drawn, or otherwise depicted whatever they believed to be worthy of remembrance. They did so to ensure that their know-how would not be lost, benefitting both present and future generations. Sketches by famous Leonardo Da Vinci, the thoughts of Marcus Aurelius, Plato's priceless writings, and Socrates' numerous notes are just a few examples of this. The Bible itself consists of passages – first shared in oral form and then in writing – featuring the Lord's Will.

As we have seen, with writing being one of the greatest inventions, remember that:

Reading is a key component to
becoming a better version of yourself,
starting from within.

Reading allows us to absorb others' wisdom and make it our own. A long time ago, there was little or no technology at all at our disposal, so people used to read quite a lot to pass time. Today, the story is very different. Overwhelmed by technology and all manner of distractions, people complain about having no time to do what they would like to do, never mind reading. They blame society for their lives being too hectic and fast-paced, but hardly ever point the finger at themselves for hitting the snooze button or wasting too much time on social media.

Personally, I have always appreciated reading, especially during summer vacations. While others spent their time collecting sports figurines, I used to spend money and time on novels. As money was low, I was going to the library to read books for free. Being an introvert by nature, reading was also a chance to escape reality. This made me more isolated, that's true, but there were also some perks. While my peers took up smoking and spent time watching football on TV, I used up the same amount of time reading and soaking up the inner messages from the great Classics. This is how I built up my fundamentals, the same that would be of huge benefit to my future self.

If you want to become successful, soak up some great books.

When prominent individuals write something of note, whether today or in the past, their wisdom remains intact within the lines of their pieces of writing. So even if they are dead and buried by now, their thinking and ideas remain alive through the centuries. Usually, the goal of writing is to transmit something to an audience: general information, daily news, and so on. Now, living in an era when printing is common and inexpensive, we print out pretty much anything from an endless range of topics: from fantasy, to horror, to self-help, drama, but also sports, weekly magazines, and romance novels. As a result, there is plenty of choice as far as reading is concerned. Similarly, what we let into our minds can deeply condition and influence us in terms of thoughts and belief formation. So in some ways, books really can make a difference in the way we shape our lives. That said, you should be very careful what you let into your mind. Try to avoid any information that is of no use to your growth.

I am saying this because in this post-modern age, outward looks take a primary position and trivialities play the real hero. The outcome? A superficial population who focuses more on appearances over values such as friendship, dignity, and respect. We embrace foolish trends just to feel accepted and buy costly gadgets to keep up with times. How much does that cost? A fortune. And to what end? Merely to impress people we don't know, and who don't care about us either.

Following the flock implies three issues:

1) to choose what's easy over what's right,
2) to prioritise instant gratification over sacrifice,
3) and last, to use one's time for trivialities, rather than working one's butt off to become a better version of yourself.

Taking the above points into account, have the courage to be different from the masses out there. Lead your energy in the right direction and make the most of your time. As Norman Vincent Peale reminds us in his book, *The Power of Positive Thinking*, "Self-knowledge is the beginning of self-correction."[4]

If you feel disoriented as to what to do or where to start, be aware that not everything is worth reading. In fact, not all books were written by wise characters. As such, like with friends and acquaintances, you should be very selective about what you choose to pick up and learn from. Time is limited and so is youth. As a result, when you carve out some time for yourself, make sure you put it to good use.

Not everyone is lucky enough to meet or interview important authors while they are still alive. Nonetheless, their important messages lie imprinted in the lines of books and can reach you wherever you are in the world. They are there, available for the taking. So, if anything, it is lack of commitment and dedication that is the real issue at the core. Unfortunately, the simple act of buying great books won't do the trick. What's in them must be read, studied, and implemented. Not coincidentally, most people own a Bible at home, but it lies unopened, covered in dust somewhere in the bookcase. Should its teachings be put into practice more often, this world would be a far better place.

When you read, make sure to follow up on the quotes and teachings you come across. Even the wisest of quotes become scrap paper if you don't act upon them. What books am I referring to? Not necessarily self-help books. It can be whatever teaches you to be a better person, starting from within. Anything highlighting the importance of respect, loyalty, friendships, and more importantly, ethics is a book worth reading.

The world we live in is such an upside-down one in which whoever cheats the most wins, whoever belittles others at school gets admired, and whoever dresses the coolest (for boys) or undresses the most (for girls) gets more likes and shares online. This is why it is critical to behave in accordance with certain values.

I took the habit of reading from my rich-minded mom. When I was sixteen, she had on her bedside table a book entitled, *The Alchemist,* first published in 1988 by Brazilian author, Paulo Coelho. Back then, despite my lack of interest in such authors or topics, she insisted I read it. Quite sceptically, I opened it and ran through the pages. I can only be grateful for that choice, as that was exactly how I started to become interested in self-improvement and becoming a better person, working from within.

While Mary was happy that I read her recommended book, Tony raised an eyebrow. To him, reading was a waste of time, while work, including homework and house chores, was everything. Raised to be hard-working, he wanted me to grow up the same as he was. I definitely agree that work is key to results. I also confirm that someone must pull their socks up if they want to raise the bar and bag achievements. *Action* is, indeed, at the root of any successful person, but – and this is a big BUT– there is something to point out:

Working SMARTER is clever.
Working HARDER is not.

The quantity of hours spent on a task is not necessarily synonymous with efficiency, let alone success. Back at school, when going to the library, I could spot so many students procrastinating, over-surfing the Net rather than focusing on their books and essays. They may have entered the library in the morning and left it in the evening, but their actual level of work was roughly two to three hours per day. The same goes with people who go to class, join a seminar, sign up for a course, and passively listen to the professor without taking any notes. They do so, believing that printing out the slides later on, or any online material, will be enough to pass the exam. That may be enough to get a decent grade, but during the class the teacher may provide interesting examples or more in-depth explanations that the slides would never include. It is usually down-to-earth examples that save a lot of work and let one understand even the most difficult concepts. By contrast, books and slides alone may not provide the same clarity. If you are a student yourself, you probably know what I am talking about.

Working smartly consists of working less, even a couple of hours, where you are fully focused on what you are doing. No chit-chatting, no phone, no social media – nothing of the sort. In case you need the Internet, it should be used only for research. If you run a marathon, how many chances do you have to hit the finish line within reasonable times if you stop every couple of miles to check your phone, chat with a friend, or have a snack? This is why the number of hours spent at your desk at work, school, in a library, or the like, is no guarantee of productivity at all.

For my poor-minded dad, there was no way he could understand the concept of working less but smartly, so that he would enjoy the rest of the day for other things. To him, working more, like ten hours straight, meant more things were done. This can be the case for manual jobs, but again, when working badly or poorly, where does the cleverness of quantity lie? This is why a quality, distraction-free job should be the privileged route, not working endless hours, maybe unfocused, or surrounded by all kinds of distractions.

When I was a teenager, Tony made it a weekend rule that I would clean the house. All in all, discipline also consists of taking care of one's place, so I can partly agree on that. The only issue was that once I had done the housework, he would ask me to deal with the garden, and then help out anywhere else. So yeah, to him, being off school meant being occupied in any way possible. If I wasn't, that would have been wasted time. Again, having an old-school background, my dad would not stand seeing me sitting around all day, or playing on the console, or reading; yes, to him, reading was the equivalent of having nothing better to do.

Strangely enough, on the one hand, my rich-minded mom was encouraging me to read, widen my horizons and possibly learn something from it. On the other hand, my poor-minded dad would only consider work or school to be worthy activities. Result? If I wanted to read, I had to do it when he was not around.

Coming back to *what* to read, I don't mean any books, but the right ones that are key to getting the right input to reorganize one's thinking. It is wise to learn from the best in the field of time-management, smart productivity, and efficiency. In short, learn how to become a better person both inside and outside. The outside reflects our inner world, so remember to work on your inner self first, your poor habits, your flaws, your weak points. These are the areas you should mostly focus on. Only then can you hope to see some sort of improvements in your outer world.

Similarly, when learning a new trade on your own, or with your family, consider the fact that it might not be the smartest one for yourself. For instance, learning to drive from one's parents can be very different from an instructor's lesson. The parent might have a lot of practice, yes, but the instructor also knows all the rules, and they know why some things should be done in a specific way, especially if you want the car engine to last longer. This is why it is always better to get trained by an experienced or competent person during any learning phase, rather than risking learning incorrectly, or wrongly, or averagely from someone with no theoretical basics at all.

To sum up, learn from the best. Both books and people are fine, as long as you soak up knowledge from those who can better you. Only then will you raise the bar in terms of thinking, knowledge, and wisdom. Only then will you lead yourself to be above average. And only then will you become successful and go places.

Be a rich-minded person (and parent) yourself:

We are constantly surrounded by people who say that we won't make it, or that our efforts are in vain, and not time worthy. They tell us to give up and try something easier. Mistakenly, they think that their limits also must necessarily be our limits. Nothing could be further from the truth. The same goes for reading. If someone doesn't read and considers it a waste of time, do not listen to them. Reading the right books can give you invaluable input and ideas for the future, but it is up to you to implement them. Filter out dream-killers as soon as possible. Let their negative talk fall on deaf ears. Your goals and time are too important to be killed by the small-minded. This also includes poor-minded parents. Even if our close friends and parents want only the best for us, it is not always guaranteed that whatever they recommend is in our best interest. If you are at school or work, and want to surround yourself with people, make sure it is those who have already achieved what you would like to achieve. Who better to show you the right way?

TRAVELLING

"Life doesn't always give you what you ask for,
but it always gives you what you need."
—Robin Sharma, author, leadership expert

On countless occasions, we try so hard to do what is in our minds. We aim to lose a few pounds, change a toxic job, study for a difficult exam, but then the results are not as expected. We lose confidence, take a step back, and promise ourselves to not do it again. Why so? Instinctively, we believe we are not good enough, not ready yet, not strong enough, not _____[fill in the blank].

This is called self-sabotage. When our will falls short and becomes unstable, we feel unsafe and, like on a battlefield, we'd rather fall back than advance. This is how we miss an incredible number of opportunities that would raise us above average, if only we dared more and pushed more. But no! What's the point if, deep down, we already believe we won't make it?

Making assumptions is the quickest way to failure and the most efficient way to staying as we are. Presuming that we won't pull it off is actually the real reason we don't make it in the end. We don't even try, or if we do, we tiptoe. We may give it a go, but then complain if the outcome is disappointing. Well, in case you didn't notice, half-stepping has never brought about anything of note. In a nutshell, you need to give it all you've got, and play full out:

Being in "negative mode" is of no use.
If anything, it clips your own wings.

Some may argue that they are not negative, but realistic. They claim that they see things as they really are under the surface. This might be true, but only in part. Understandably, while some things may go wrong, it is a different story to say that if we try, it will necessarily go wrong – and not once or twice, but all the freaking time!

Being driven by emotions, we are weak. We may have collected a number of negative experiences beforehand, to the point of influencing our subconscious to believe that if we dare again, by default, it won't work. Then we feel down again and suffer again. This is how we develop the terrible habit of seeing the half-empty glass everywhere. We presume that we are always missing something in order to succeed, while instead, what we really lack is this: 1) a bit of courage for what the future holds, and 2) the ability to leave the past in its rightful place – in the past, a place to visit, but not to dwell.

Like the great majority, I was also into negative thinking anytime I expected to pass a test or achieve the grade that I wanted. My entry test at university is a case in point. After high school, it was my intention to enter the faculty of interpretation and translation. In addition, I had worked all summer to save up enough to finance myself. Mentally, I was already picturing myself at university, socializing with my new mates. As naïve as I was back then, I thought that the mere intention was enough to pull it off, and that proper revision and working hard during the summer were sufficient to overcome the obstacle. How wrong I was. Being the entry test as hard as anything, I didn't pass it. This is when the world collapsed on me. This is also when I learned a life lesson first-hand: the world owes us nothing. Simply put, no matter how hard we try, or slave away, or how good we are to people, there is still no guarantee of success with our plans. Also, I learned that "life doesn't always give you what you ask for," as Robin Sharma puts it in his book, *The Monk Who Sold His Ferrari*. However, Sharma says, "…it always gives you what you need."[5] This is such a big truth, but it is not always crystal clear in the moment. That is, when something goes wrong, and we are without a back-up plan, how easy is that to accept? Not too easy.

At the time, I was eighteen, and I could not find an explanation for the injustice that had just struck me. I could not understand why life suddenly turned its back on me, despite all my good will, hard work, and excellent grades from high school. In fact, the only clear explanation I could find was damn misfortune. Only a few years later would I understand that life was putting me to the test. I was not ready to go to university straight away, without first growing up as a person.

That would become clear later, but it was "clear as mud" back then. To me, it was all bad luck, and without a back-up plan to rely on, I was left high and dry. I had just finished my summer job as a waiter, and without university,

I didn't know what to do. Unable to find a way out, I took a gap year, just to reflect and to get to know myself better. It is curious that we usually spend lots of time to get to know others better, but never enough time to get to know ourselves better. We rarely ask ourselves critical questions such as:

1. Who and what am I at this point in my life?

2. Am I satisfied with my life? If not, what should I change?

3. Am I happy at the moment? If not, what should I turn upside down so I can smile again?

We can ask ourselves these questions, like many others, with the specific purpose of seeing our current status as people –personally, emotionally, professionally, and sentimentally.

I spent too many comfortable years at high school without ever minding any of the above questions. I never learned what I really wanted, spotted my personal strengths, nor did I work my butt off on my weaknesses. I took this chance during my gap year to get to know myself better and make up for the lost time.

Tony was dead set against my plan. To him, one gap year equated to 365 days of wasted time. He feared it would take me longer to finish my studies compared to my peers. *Well,* I said to myself, *what's the point of starting a faculty, and maybe dropping out because I didn't like it?* Also, I didn't care about my peers. They were free to do what they liked, and so was I. My rich-minded mom thought as I did. It was indeed better to choose a field after due consideration, rather than making any hasty decisions, and this happened to be truer than expected. In fact, many of my former schoolmates made quick decisions and enrolled straightaway in economics, law, archaeology, etc., only to withdraw at the end of the first year.

In my view, that was the real waste, in terms of time, money and energy. Some might disagree on this. Well, while it is true that learning is never a waste of time, we cannot say the same for the money and energy that were depleted, never to be replaced. To Tony, the only important issue was that I would be employed, no matter what I chose. Being exhausted by the summer season, due to an average of sixty working hours a week, there was no way I would start working straight after the summer if I didn't choose to study. In need of proper rest and to reflect on my future ahead, I made up my mind, took a gap year, and travelled instead.

My rich-minded mom also travelled in her twenties, so she supported this plan of mine. After all, if that could make my mind clearer, she saw no reason to be against it. The one who was opposed to the idea was my poor-minded dad. Considering any recreational activities to be a waste of time and money, he agreed on my resting a bit, but without necessarily travelling. He would say things like, "Why do you want to burn the money you've earned so far? If you want to travel, go see your grandparents; that's definitely risk-free and cheap in comparison." That was his idea of a holiday – visiting one's relatives or going on a trip to the near seaside.

Giving it some thought, that would have been easier, safer, and pocket-friendly in comparison. Staying with my own people, however, would neither allow me to properly reflect on my future, nor would it allow me to be out of that bloody comfort zone that was preventing me from really growing. Also, visiting one's relatives is not really my idea of travelling. Maybe attending a nice gathering was okay, but that is all.

Instead, what I really needed was just to be on my own. It is not within the scope of this book to go through all my time abroad, describing both places and people I encountered. What is important, though, is what I learned along the way. The greatest lesson I picked up was not to judge others because of their diversity. In fact, some trends, habits, and ways of living may be out-of-place in one country, but the norm in another. So, who are we to judge? Or worse, who are we to look down on those who are different from us? For instance, Italian people I knew would pay particular attention to the way they dressed. Abroad, everyone was dressing as they pleased, more out of comfort than anything. The same applied to eating habits. It is the norm to have a sweet breakfast in Italy, but I could see how many people elsewhere preferred a savory one early in the morning. Again, who are we to judge, when looking at others and their lifestyles?

I will tell you who: A fixed-minded person would judge.

One priceless lesson I learned was to embrace diversity, rather than criticizing it. I was curious and willing to learn from others, beginning with the language and local slang. Over time, I also started to question my own ways and learned new, different ones. This is what I called real richness, starting from within, judging less to embrace more, dare more, LIVE MORE. This is how I changed my habits, starting with food, and became a citizen of the world, rather than just a citizen of only one country:

Being flexible opens up an entire
world of opportunities, but only for
those who don't have tunnel vision.

It is noteworthy to say that there is an abundance of opportunities out there, available to all those who have the right mindset to spot them and, more importantly, grab them. Unfortunately, most good chances remain undiscovered, because most people don't have the right mental approach to perceive them when passing by. Blinded by comfort and ease, they just pass by them as if nothing happened. This is how a minority of individuals get a lot out of life, versus others – the majority – who pick up very little; it is those who enjoy the lion's share versus those who have only peanuts.

It is not a matter of luck or greed. Rather, it is having the right mental attitude and taking calculated risks versus staying in one's comfort zone. In this case, the former are more likely to spot and grab any good opportunities lying ahead. The latter would still see the same opportunity, but because they are used to always seeing what may go wrong, they are likely to turn around and go the other way, or retreat, instead:

Spotting opportunities everywhere is a habit,
but the same goes for obstacles.

The flexible person finds it normal to spot opportunities anytime they look. How? It's not that they imagine how something presents itself in the moment, but how it could be in the future. If they see a car or a house in ruin, they don't see it as a write-off. Rather, they visualize what that car or building could become one day. And this is how they spend little money and close very good deals. Being flexible and imaginative are key to a world of possibilities. The fixed-minded, by contrast, will spot the same car or house, but because they are used to seeing the half-empty glass, they are very likely to dismiss them as something not worth their time, money, and effort. Why?

Because they see and evaluate things by their current state, rather than going beyond the physical.

Travelling was critical to making me become a flexibly minded person. It taught me to take risks, but also to persist when something took longer than expected. You cannot imagine, by adopting this approach, how many things are actually possible. Finding good deals for next to nothing, studying what you like, and doing a job you are passionate about are just a few examples. All you need to do is be open enough and determined enough. Do so, and you won't be disappointed:

> ***Seize the day to avoid the day seizing you with unexpected circumstances.***

Be a rich-minded person (and parent) yourself:

Travel to become more flexible and resilient. Do this and you will stop seeing things as only black-and-white. Those who give up too easily or quickly, like in nature, are not expected to enjoy the big slice of the cake. All they are likely to get is the crumbs. This is exactly what happens to most of us. Out of fear, laziness, or simply lack of backbone, we tiptoe, or do the bare minimum, just to make it to the end of the month. We are not in control of the situation ahead, and we let others decide for us (our superiors, the government, global crises, etc.). When you shut down others (starting with the TV and mindless internet), you automatically have more time, focus, and control for yourself. This is when you get to know yourself better, and you can grab life by the horns again. When you decide for yourself, you seize the day. And when you do so, you become unstoppable. Never again will outer circumstances push you around.

AMBITIONS

"Life has no limitations,
except the ones you make."
—Les Brown, motivational speaker,
former Ohio politician

Having a purpose in life is something everyone should have. "Should" because, as far as the eye can see, too many feel lost and disoriented and don't have a clear goal to pursue. This holds true especially for Millennials and the Gen Zers. Not a single generation has ever had as many opportunities as the above. Social media, YouTube®, and the Internet as a whole provide ways of becoming well-known. Yet, there is something current generations struggle with a lot: *consistency* – picking a road and sticking to it long enough to come to fruition. They also struggle because they are overwhelmed with opportunities. This seems a paradox, but that's the way it is. Sometimes, having many open doors can be a disadvantage. Why? Because it can easily take you off track, preventing you from persevering with a particular objective.

Too undecided to select a single route and stay with it long enough to enjoy its fruits, the majority tiptoe around possibilities. The only issue is that just "giving it a try," or trying a bit of this and a bit of that won't take you anywhere. In fact, the mere attempts do not imply real commitment, never mind persistence. Without these two ingredients – taking a single route and staying with it long enough – nothing concrete is likely to pan out.

Due to the abundance of possibilities, it is also true that all too many individuals and parents choose the easiest options. They go for the road that doesn't break a sweat, where guarantees are visible from the start. This is usually the preferred path for many, including my poor-minded dad. This is the route with the map that states: "Study hard, find a steady job, and retire." This is the reason universities are packed with students. Pushed by their parents, they enroll in the hope of getting good marks that will let them slot easily into the job market.

If you recall from earlier, I had decided to take a gap year by travelling abroad, not only to earn some money, but also to think over my future more carefully. Additionally, I saw and lived through a number of events that I could have never experienced by staying in the place Tony didn't want me to leave – in my town, or "in my own shell," to put it better. This made me become a sharper observer, seeing things from a more well-rounded perspective, and also made me more flexibly minded. This was the same flexibility that my mother possessed when she also travelled at a young age.

More important, I understood that when one wants to achieve something, there are multiple ways of doing so. I know a lot of people who have only one method, which is trying harder, doing more of the same. For instance, to earn more money, many businesses would expand their operating hours. This is a very common practice, and logically, most would head toward it like ducks to water. While it is true that being open or on call longer might give you more customers, the reality is that you are working the same, just over a longer span of time. Instead, if you identify the hours when you work most, you can exploit that time by increasing your quality and becoming very good at a key area like marketing – spotting what the customer wants, and then not only living up to their expectations, but also delighting them by giving them more than they expect. In doing so, you can work half as long, and still have the same money, or even more.

This is because you work not longer, but smarter. You concentrate your workload into your peak time, during which you work your butt off and give your best in terms of quality and results. That is where most of your income should come from. The same happens in the office. You can complete the same workload in half the time, if you have a distraction-free environment and the determination to get the job done without too many chats or breaks in-between.

Another example is diet. Some people wrongly conclude that the only way to get back in shape is through the consumption of low-calorie foods or zero-sugar soft drinks. That's a black-and-white approach. There are, in fact, tons of efficient methods to get back in shape, including taking long walks, or cycling (even on the way to work), choosing the stairs over the elevator, or eating less food, but of higher quality.

Seeing things from more perspectives is good for the mind because it makes you flexible to the point of not panicking when something goes wrong. Also, it makes you realize that if one way does not pay off, or does not pay off any longer, another way must be put in place if you don't want to fall behind and be left behind. Too many are chained to the same old method that has saved the day for years, but suddenly feel lost if it doesn't work any longer due to external changes.

An approach I really like is to do things little by little, taking a small step at a time in order to build great results in the long run. Taking the above example, I would remain fit not by working out at the gym or at home exclusively, but I would walk more often outdoors, and take the stairs at least once a day. Also, I would eat better and eliminate all those foods that are tasty, but not very nutritious. So, little sacrifices over an extended period of time can really do wonders. The same goes for many other areas. When sending out job applications, I would make a point of sending out three CVs a day, every day, making it an average of over twenty a week. This is by far more effective than randomly sending out tons of them in the first few days, and then waiting for an answer.

Becoming a better observer of your surroundings, and a more flexible thinker, will bring about numerous benefits, and require less struggle for your future choices. When we make a bad decision, it is mostly due to being too hasty or impulsive. If only we took some time to reflect and better analyze the circumstances, we wouldn't trip or fall as many times.

Other than that, by living abroad, and putting myself to the test several times, I would summarize the whole experience this way:

There are many ways to obtain the same goals;
it is not just one approach or nothing.

For a great many people, it is one way – their way – or nothing. If they did something, but for one reason or another it didn't work, oftentimes they mistakenly believe they are not good enough, smart enough, ready enough, or the like. This is a shame, really. It is not about skills. If anything, it is about finding the correct approach to deal with an already determined or limited situation. I would like to reassure you that no one is a born failure. You may need to correct your ways or plans, but everyone can make it eventually. The difference lies in being persistent when things get tough, and humble enough to experiment with more approaches to get to the final stage. Experimenting with more methods is fundamental. If one way does not work, do yourself a favor and don't give up. Tweak your approach, try another one, and then another, until you find the one most suitable for you and your needs.

For instance, one can learn a new language in more than one way. At university, many of my peers in my course and I were learning foreign languages in order to pass the exams, but in class we were merely doing grammar, exercises, and a bit of speaking. That was all. Because I was not satisfied with it, I implemented my approach by watching movies in the original language with the subtitles. This is how I learned lots of lexicon and pronunciation straight from native speakers. In addition, I looked for Erasmus students, which are foreign students on an exchange program, with whom to practice speaking, along with picking up any colloquial words and idioms. Not surprisingly, I never had problems in passing my language exams. Having many resources at my disposal to count on, besides just the teacher and the books, I was well-equipped with the sufficient knowledge to pass any test. In contrast, I saw first-hand many of my mates failing because they were relying only on the knowledge from the course and the teacher. Not surprisingly, they got average marks. Taking all this into account, implant this into your head:

> *When one does the bare minimum, one gets*
> *a minimal result, but when one works hard*
> *and experiments with more methods,*
> *great results lie ahead.*

It is all a matter of ambitions and what one aims for. It is not about having luck or possessing some special talents. Anyone is able to achieve great results, provided that they do their best, work hard consistently, and are flexible with their approaches.

You see, sometimes doing one's best won't necessarily put the victory in the bag, despite many books claiming this is so. I mean, doing one's best can certainly increase your chances of success, but that's an incomplete formula.

Since anything we do is a journey, consistency and flexibility will eventually make a difference in whatever we do. And like any journey, we are constantly faced with bumps and turns. Taking detours along the way is critical to seeing the light at the end of the tunnel.

If you feel stuck or lost, remind yourself to experiment with more than one method. If one way does not work, take the courage to change your approach, despite having been taught just one way in your heyday. This may save you lots of time, money, and effort.

You may once have noticed a fly bouncing insistently against a glass pane, hoping to get out. The little animal does so because that's the only way it knows, *repetition*. Sadly, that's not a winning strategy. That won't let out the fly for sure, no matter the effort. The same goes for real life. So many individuals and parents only know one way, one method, and mistakenly think that pressing will guarantee them victory. That is just WRONG! Having that kind of approach can only cause a series of defeats, with the result of doubting themselves, their means, and their own capacities. It is not the fact that they are incapable, or not skilled enough, even if tons of people believe so; it is just a matter of flexibility. They must keep on trying, yes, but by using a variety of ways, if their own have proved to be inefficient. So, if the fly stopped bouncing against the glass and gave it some thought, it would realize that it should either examine the whole window first, or look for an adjacent one in order to find a way out. The same goes with students. If their way-of-doing-things does not pay off, or does not turn out as expected, they consider themselves limited, or simply unlucky. This is also a false belief. As Les Brown reminds us, "Life has no limitations, except for the ones you make."[6] Most billionaires today are self-made. They obtained (and still do) incredible wealth by themselves, not by inheritance. Along with Les Brown, they too believed that life has no limits. Result? Look at the empires many have built up.

This was rocket science to my poor-minded dad. He would either try one method, usually his own from the past, and if it didn't work, he would either try harder and harder by using the same ways, or simply sit back and give up.

For example, if working hard at his restaurant would not provide enough turnover, Tony would blame the world crisis, the competitors, or conclude that people were simply not hungry. He would choose to stay open longer hours, or budget more strictly on ingredients to make ends meet. If we look at most corporations, it is common practice to be tight on budgets and let employees go to play on the defense, but matches are never won that way; they are won by attacking, not defending. Unfortunately, the above route has always been the one the masses have preferred. If things get tough, people choose to play it safe. They do not realize that by making cuts here and there, there is always a price to pay, and that price is usually quality and employee retention. Of course, when quality goes missing, customers leave. The same happened to Tony. Having decreased the quality to make ends meet, he lost a tremendous number of regular customers. What was his reaction? He simply blamed anything and anyone but himself.

To my dad, limitations were always due to external circumstances like the economic crisis, the lack of customers, or even the harsh competition. He would not understand that tweaking his current methods, and concentrating more on quality and marketing, would not only be enough to bounce back, but also to earn even more than before. Because, to use Les Brown's words once again, "Life has no limitations, except the ones you make."

Life is full of opportunities, but only to those who can perceive them. Stressing this point is fundamental to having a fulfilling existence. Abundance is our birth right. There is no such thing as a lack of possibilities. However, the great majority don't realise this. They believe that there are obstacles lurking everywhere, some sort of dark forces in place that prevent them from obtaining what they really want. By repeating this mantra again and again, this is the reality they create in their own minds. And because the mind is so powerful, what is repeated non-stop becomes a reality. This is essentially how we create our own invisible cages around us. This is also how so many people lead an unhappy life. They live in scarcity and say things like, "There is not enough for everyone," "Life is too tough and full of obstacles," etc. Having piled up these limiting beliefs, they try to survive in this tough reality, as they call it. The same rang true for Tony. He deduced that most of his working life was a mere rat race, made up of paying bills, and trying to make ends meet. Convinced that life was hard and limited by itself, he was trying to pass on his pessimistic supposition to me. And for many years, I mistakenly believed that I was unlucky, not clever enough, not skilled enough, and so on, while instead all I was doing was creating a rubbish reality by reasoning the wrong way. Because of that, I missed many golden opportunities:

Life is only limited and scarce if we believe it is.
Likewise, it is abundant and rich if we are convinced so, too.

Be a rich-minded person (and parent) yourself:

Have a goal, but don't limit yourself to one method to achieving it. Also, when it comes to your objectives, set no limitations. If you have any doubts, it is probably due to fear or lack of self-confidence. You don't have to continue down that road. Convince yourself that you are worthy, that you deserve it! Limitations may be acceptable to others, but should never be the norm to you. Sadly, we are surrounded with people who wear blinders, individuals who can easily put us down with their own thinking; this is even worse when they come from our family, or group of close friends. The good news is that *you* are neither your family, nor your friends. You are you and they are themselves. This means that their limitations are theirs, but don't necessarily need to be yours, too. When you realize that there are no real boundaries, except the ones you make, a whole new world of possibilities awaits you. Don't wait too long. Life is too short, and so is youth. So, what's the point of wasting it through endless waiting and procrastinating?

SETTLING FOR LESS

"Know who you are. Know what you want.
Know what you deserve. And don't settle for less."
—Tony Gaskins, author, motivational speaker, life coach

Having dreams has always been a trait of human beings. In their prime, many boys and girls dream of becoming sports champions, astronauts, and movie stars. What do they have in common? Exactly. They think big! They have no limiting beliefs to put them down and keep them down. Now, aspiring is not a bad thing, nor something to be ashamed of. So, why do we blame a person when they daydream? Why laugh when one says they will become famous, or a millionaire, or a VIP one day, or when they insist that the projects or inventions in their heads will change the world? Sadly, ambition comes at a price. Not by chance or historical flukes, ambitious people have always been laughed at, or labelled as crazy weirdos. How so? Simply because we are so accustomed to settling for less, being realistic, and only counting on what's available and visible before us. As stated earlier, we choose from the menu of the available possibilities, rather than making up our minds and creating our own. Steve Jobs was definitely a visionary when he forecasted that computers would revolutionize the workplace, and so too were Thomas Edison, Leonardo da Vinci, the Wright brothers, Marie Curie, and many others. Why is it, then, that we are so used to settling for less? Why are we okay with realizing less than our infinite possibilities, brains and talents permit?

According to research, we tend to become what is around us. It is not so hard to believe when scientists say we are similar to the environment we grow up in. Over time, it is just natural that we become part of our surroundings, in terms of behavior, people, even our way of thinking, if you will. This is the outcome of what and with whom we are mostly in contact.

Everyone is different, you may argue. That is true, but I can provide a personal example to elaborate on the above. I have always found it difficult to properly study at home. I was surrounded by all sorts of distractions (the sofa, the fridge, screens, etc.) and this made it arduous for me to remain focused. As a result, I had to leave the house (my environment), choosing a different one, in my case, the library, in order to really get down to work. Being surrounded by books and total quiet, I became a model student, something I could never have achieved back at home surrounded by all kinds of distractions. The same holds true with people. When I started going deep into motivation and self-improvement, as I have already discussed in my previous book, *The Greatest Version of Yourself: A Journey Within*, slowly but surely I dropped most of my friends, as they were mediocre in terms of thinking, ambitions, and future in general, and I found new ones along the way. I befriended men and women who were more prone to talking about self-fulfilment and true happiness. As with books, this is when I started being very selective about the friends and acquaintances with whom I surrounded myself. As a side note, although I could be selective with people, acquiring and dropping whom I desired, I could not do the same with my own family. Family is family, after all. You have one and cannot pick and choose your family members at will. Sometimes, we wish we could, but this is just not doable.

This also regarded my poor-minded dad. Despite giving me all sorts of old-fashioned advice due to his poor mindset and background, I could not point-blank kick him out of the house. Rather, I was forced to stay under the same roof, having him around all the time. This is how I ran into very differing views on topics such as hobbies, people, school, and so on. Not surprisingly, I got really confused for many years. Having two parents in discord with pretty much anything, for a long time I could not make up my mind as to who and what to listen to, or not. One of the most recurrent topics of conversation for my parents was money. When people say that money does not buy happiness, I dare to disagree for a few reasons. Money may not acquire happiness on a superficial level, but if we see it from a deeper perspective, having money on the side (ethically earned, of course), gives you the opportunity to work less and to concentrate more on your passions and hobbies. Also, it allows you to travel more and get to know yourself better:

It is when we carve out more time for ourselves that life becomes truly beautiful.

Likewise, working does not buy happiness either, but again, the quality of the jobs we do on a daily basis is critical to our general mood and well-being. If we have a job that we like, we are more likely to wake up satisfied and be content to start the day ahead. By contrast, when we have an occupation we dislike, it becomes very hard to put on a smile and jumpstart the day in an optimistic way. Some may say this is subjective. Maybe yes, maybe not. What I know for sure is that it is just psychological that when we do an activity we like, we are more likely to repeat it again and again. Whereas, when we do something we hate, or are surrounded by people we can't stand, it becomes very hard to repeat the activity. Because work is an integral part of our lives, this is when LIFE BECOMES MISERABLE, and we lead an unhappy existence for the best part of our waking hours.

While Mary agreed that we need to have a job that we like in order to feel good in general, leading a satisfying existence as a result, Tony thought differently, as always. For him, any job was all right, provided that it was paid, regardless of its quality or working conditions. His thinking being behind the times, and as a proud father, he wanted to pass his ideas on to me. I have many friends (cousins included) who, regrettably, chose to listen to their parents about having a safe paycheck and a permanent job, rather than spending more time to find an occupation more up to their expectations, and thus more pleasant. How about an occupation that would pay less at first, but that would definitely pay dividends in the long run? Nope, for the majority with tunnel vision, the short-term is all that matters. This would explain why so many of us have a job we don't like, but are resistant to take the risk of dropping it for something better.

It is because of the short-term benefits, especially easy money, that we habitually settle for less. This is how we work and work, but keep our talents dormant for our whole lives, thus leaving them unused. It is such a pity that the guy I previously referred to will never exploit his excellence for drawing, and that he just keeps it as a hobby. And it is a shame that another woman I know who is an excellent gymnast keeps her skills only as an extracurricular activity due to her daily duties. I ignore why they made the choices they have made, but hypothetically, let's say, they both had poor-minded parents who gave them poor-minded recommendations, in terms of choices for their future. Result? They followed through on what their parents said, and now have jobs below their potential and talent.

This is the reason I came to a point where I was so stubborn and determined to ignore Tony, and just listened to Mary's advice. Having worked in hospitality for a good number of summers, by the end of high school I chose to no longer listen to my dad. Despite being occupied, having a paycheck and receiving good tips, I was continually dissatisfied to the core because I wasn't fulfilled. Doing the same things again and again, just for the sake of money, was not living at all. Rather, it was half-living, nothing more, nothing less.

Through personal experience and rubbish jobs, I learned first-hand the importance of feeling fulfilled inside. Money was not the primary aspect for me when looking for work. Job satisfaction is critical to living a happy life, as we spend most of our years in the workplace. But this was not the case for Tony. To him, that was mere daydreaming. He believed that we cannot always have what we want, and that we all would like to dream and build sandcastles, but reality is a different story. He preached that we have to settle for what is around us. This is exactly what he did for the sake of money and a secure paycheck, but to the detriment of his happiness and overall personal satisfaction. By contrast, Mary would have never sacrificed happiness for money. For my own sake, she would recommend I keep on looking for what made me feel good, and more importantly, *fulfilled*. She taught me not to sell myself short and select an easy route, but to create my own new one, if necessary. In short, while one parent would say to play it safe, the other would give it her all.

This is how I went to university and later moved abroad to work. As I could not find what I was looking for in my town, I left to look for it elsewhere. That turned out to be one of the wisest things I have ever done. It was not easy, especially at first. Everything was new to me, not to mention the fact that I had no friends or relatives to count on, but the reward for doing so turned out to be priceless. I had more chances and a wider menu of options to choose from.

Even now, many years later, Mary's teachings have benefitted me. I have a job that I like. I don't mind Mondays or waking up early in the morning. Had I followed my poor-minded dad, I may now have a decently paying job near my place, but I would almost surely feel bored and unfulfilled. Financially safe, yes, but deeply dissatisfied at my core. As for you, dear reader, if it is Monday or Tuesday, and you already long for the weekend, this should be an alarm bell for you. This is when something is really going wrong and you should change it accordingly. Trust me, it is not normal to resist waking up and, even less ordinary, to hate the first days of the week. If you hate your life deep down, then something must change.

If you hate your current condition as a parent or worker, it is possible that you listened to some bad tips many years earlier and took wrong turns accordingly. If that is your case, you are not alone. This happens to thousands of people worldwide every day. It also happened to me more than once, back in the day. If I have a job that I like now, regardless of money or benefits, it is because I had the determination to look for one, without ever giving up before rejections by recruiters. I didn't settle for less and I created my own possibilities, like Mary taught me to.

What about Plan B? Having a back-up plan is like a safety net. People feel safe when they know from the start that a parachute will save them, if necessary. The so-called safety net, however comfortable it may be, comes at a price. It makes people feel more relaxed, and they take it easy as a result. Personally, I don't like Plan B, because I know I am not really committed if I know straight up that I won't end up empty-handed if I screw up. In fact, it is when there are no precautions at all that you can't allow yourself to mess up. This is when you start taking things very seriously and give them all you've got. It is usually in circumstances like this that miracles happen. This is when things that you thought were impossible suddenly become possible.

In his book, *Think and Grow Rich,* Napoleon Hill speaks of a captain who went to war with his army. Before facing the enemy, he did something that was unheard-of. Suicidal, if you like. He burnt the bridges behind him to the ground. In doing so, should things take a bad turn, there would be no escape for him and his men. All they had to do to go home unscathed was to face the enemy head-on and down to their last ounce of energy. When it is a matter of life and death, no one would simply "try" to stay alive; they would give one hundred percent to save their skin. Of course, nowadays we live in a civilised world, with laws and human rights. In most cases in the Western World, people don't face life-or-death matters any longer. However, they are likely to face situations when real money is at stake. When debts and bankruptcy loom on the horizon, this is when people open their eyes and show more commitment and seriousness. Implementing more of these two attributes can't help but enhance the chances to pull it off.

As this chapter comes to an end, remember that we should never settle for less. With all of us possessing some talents and skills, the least we should do is to do them justice by putting them to use. We are capable of great things, if we really are serious about our resolutions.

Be a rich-minded person (and parent) yourself:

Settling for less is a losing strategy. It may give you what you need in the moment; that is, money and stability. In the long-term, it brings about a price to pay: personal satisfaction and fulfilment. Compromise will mean that you always have something in the bag, true, but ask yourself: is it what you really want? A rich-minded person (or parent) would never teach you to settle. He or she would pass on the idea to fight for your ideas and space in society, and to lead the way, rather than letting life shake you around according to the circumstances. Be mindful of this next time you hear your family or relatives say, "Be happy as you are."

REPEATED MISTAKES

"Take chances, make mistakes.
That's how you grow."
—**Mary Tyler Moore, award-winning actress, producer and social advocate**

Today's world is not perfect. As individuals, we have all sorts of flaws and imperfections. I, for one, am a firm believer that perfection is unattainable. That said, everyone should at least do their best if they want to be fulfilled and achieve lasting happiness. Falling down is normal, but repeatedly hitting the same wall is not. I am not talking about mistakes that are different from one another; I am focusing on hiccups that we continually experience, without ever learning anything behind:

Life is willing to teach lessons,
but only to those who are willing to learn.

When it rains, we instinctively cover up, and remember to bring an umbrella along with us next time. When the conductor catches us without a valid ticket on the train, we make a point of buying the ticket next time. And finally, when we eat something bad and feel sick, we become more selective about what we gobble down in the future.

Who would appreciate getting fined or soaked on a continuous basis? No one, of course. And who would like continuous food poisoning? Again, nobody. Yet, this is what happens to the majority of people daily. Some speed, despite knowing they should not. Others drink more than they can handle, just to let their hair down. And others keep smoking as a stressbuster, despite knowing very well how detrimental it can be to their health. Unlike animals that avoid risks by instinct, humans tend to make the same mistakes again and again, despite being aware of their side effects and possible consequences. Do some simply lack brains? Maybe, but I think the matter goes deeper than that.

When they say, "It is fine to hit a snag," – the normal price we pay for having a well-lived life – they should also add that it is worth it, as long as something gets picked up in the process. It may sound obvious, at least in theory, but in practice it is not. People still get fined, soaked, etc. They keep eating rubbish food, and turn to medicines and supplements, rather than attending to and conquering their vices at the root. They keep hitting the same glass (like the fly when trying to escape from the window), without ever realizing that a simple tweak of mindset and strategy would set them free. This would also mean less trouble and a smoother existence. Why is it that this is not happening?

Experience is there to speak to us, provided that we are willing to listen.

We fancy picking up what's easy over what's right. This is not new. When short-term pleasures are at hand, they look so appetizing and irresistible that it becomes easy to fall for them. This was a known fact to Mary, but obviously not to Tony. While my mother would consider having a good job critical to one's happiness, mood, and spirits, regardless of wage, my dad would rather trade happiness for a stable occupation, as long as it provided guarantees and long-term stability. For Tony, this usually meant neglecting personal satisfaction or decent working conditions. To him, the most important factor was steadiness and a safe pay until retirement. Some might agree with this, some not, but one thing is certain. Even now, tons of teenagers listen to the wrong parent, and follow up on whatever they say. These are the boys and girls who, for example, start working in the same place in their twenties, only to leave it for retirement. This makes a lifetime spent in the same position, at the same place, with colleagues they probably hate or a boss they can no longer stand. And all of that just "for the sake of security and stability," as Tony would put it. At what price? I will tell you at what price: to the cost of sacrificing a lifetime of potential and self-fulfilment.

Fulfilment is only possible to those to have the guts to abandon stability and a safe wage for the sake of something higher and worthier. It is only attainable by those who are in search of personal satisfaction, and want to achieve it, not only in thoughts, but also with concrete actions. Well, to these people, it will take longer to get to their destination; that's a given. If the rewards are personal satisfaction, improved mood, and less fatigue, this is absolutely worth it, in terms of time, money, and effort.

In addition, feeling satisfied with what you are doing every day is just priceless. You can benefit from fewer mood swings and less stress in general. I am saying this because it is much more stressful to perform something we dislike, compared to something we truly appreciate. Instead, when the economic factor becomes the top priority, usually one never has enough. Think of the many athletes who continuously change teams for higher pay. Think of the "Wolf of Wall Street" who never had enough of accumulating wealth. To him, money was never enough, no matter how much he piled up.

Since bad decisions cost money, time, and sometimes also tears, this is the reason why learning from previous mistakes is key to a quality life – something too precious to be left to chance. That means you should do all it takes to level up, and the only way to do so is to take the past as a great teacher, as something you can always learn from:

Visiting the past is a good thing.
Dwelling on it can be toxic and take you down.

Do not make the mistake Tony did – trading happiness and overall working satisfaction for money or any short-term benefits. If you do, you are in for some unhappy years ahead.

It is not just about work and money. We trade happiness in many other fields. We may study something we dislike just to make our parents proud. We may choose to marry the wrong person just for their financial stability. Or we may postpone a number of things until retirement, naively believing that by then we will start to really enjoy ourselves. People reasoning on these terms apparently don't realize that energy is not on "will call," nor is time. When the flame of life starts flickering, it may be too late to get around to the many projects in their minds that they never dared to get started out of fear, worry, or lack of time.

We often hear people say, "Life is now," or *carpe diem*. Yet, when it comes to action and making decisions that could give us a breakthrough, we prefer to turn our heads away. This is when life is not "now" anymore, but rather some day in the future, without ever specifying *when*. Again, we postpone so many things out of fear, worry, lack of time, or simply because we feel that we are not good enough or ready yet, so we eventually put them to bed forever. This explains why we never really start doing what we should do, preferring what's easy over what's right. Then here comes that familiar moment when excuses step in and get the better of us. We blame anything and anyone, rather than the real culprit – ourselves! We habitually sabotage ourselves through negative self-talk and bad feelings, killing any good ideas from the start. No surprise, then, that nothing ever blossoms from our minds.

Tony behaved the same way. His plan was simple: to accumulate as much money as possible in order to finally start enjoying life in retirement. What's wrong with that? Nothing really. The issue is that he was sacrificing both his family and personal life in order to achieve his goal. Having listened to many elderly people, I've found they all confirm that retirement is not as good as it seems, or as they hoped it would be. It is true that one may have more money and time at their disposal, but it is also true that they lack the energy to actually do many of the things they had planned to do earlier on. Suppose energy equated to petrol. Without it, the driver doesn't go far. Likewise, the elderly may have lots of finances and spare time to rely on, that is true, but lack the energy to really enjoy themselves – not to mention all the ailments due to aging. This is when they realize how foolish it was to postpone what they could have done much earlier in life, when they had less money and time, but definitely the initiative and the grit to rock the world. Now that they are retired, and too slow for most activities, they blame age, and time that went by too quickly. Again, we blame anything and anyone but ourselves:

Do not wait too long.
There might be no second chance.

Life is willing to teach us, provided that we are willing to learn from it. As such, keep both your eyes and ears open when moving through your life. Make a point of picking up a lesson or two from your previous mistakes, no matter how insignificant they may seem. In doing so, there's a good chance of avoiding them in the future. Also, if you want to go one step further, learn from others' mistakes as well. You don't need to damage yourself in order to learn your lessons. A very basic example is smoking. Personally, I never started because by simply looking at current smokers, I could see how detrimental it is and how hard it is to quit. Unlike animals, most people feel the need to try out new experiences at any cost, without considering the side effects. Another instance is turning to alcohol or food to get the dopamine we need to cope with daily problems and stress. Now, we all have difficult moments; no one is exempt. Hitting the bottle or polishing off the contents of the fridge, however, have never been the solution. Sure, the latter provide some sort of temporary relief, but certainly won't solve anything.

We don't necessarily need to try out new things to realize how bad they can be to both our body and health. In many cases, the world has already tested most of the activities we would like to do, so getting informed and keeping your eyes open is critical to anticipating or avoiding any foolish mistakes. This is especially true when it comes to putting money on the table. Before investing your finances in stocks, bonds, and the like, get all the necessary information, and then go for it, but take only calculated risks. Warren Buffett is very wealthy because he only invested in a few very remunerative investments. He didn't get rich with luck, but with brains and a constant, vigilant eye.

Tony was of a different opinion; he would take no risks at all, preferring the comfort zone to the big bad world. By contrast, Mary wanted me to pursue my dreams. There was a high chance I would trip up. I had almost finished high school at the time. I could have found a job quite easily due to my previous experience in hospitality, but since I wanted to do the "quality jump," this is when I decided to go abroad and create the experiences I could not have had back home. Furthermore, having failed the entry test to university and having decided to take a gap year, I considered it to be the best way forward, at least for me. Once again, I decided to listen to Mary, ignoring my father's poor advice to stay and work from home, and that turned out to be one of the best things I had ever done for myself. As this chapter ends, remember this big truth I experienced first-hand outside of my comfort zone:

In order to achieve more,
you first have to become more.

Be a rich-minded person (and parent) yourself:

When something is not good for you, be it junk food, drinking, or smoking for example, do yourself a favour: don't be tempted. Don't fall for it, especially if you did so before. We all like our comforts, but the real question is this: is it so damn necessary to damage yourself to get some short-term pleasure in the moment, whatever it may be? Of course not! Rather than healing from undesirable side effects at a later date, usually through medicines and supplements, make a point of solving the cause at the root – bad habits, poor decisions, and a weak will. If you wish to go one step further, be a close observer of your circumstances. If someone dropped their studies, and regretted it a few years later, be smart and don't follow in their footsteps. If your friends are smokers and find it very hard to quit now, what's the point of starting to smoke yourself? So many people invested in virtual coins, and got peanuts in return, or worse, they lost everything. Why copy them? Again, be alert with your surroundings. Just because those around you made poor decisions and are now paying a dear price for it, be smart and don't end up the same way as them. *Speak less, observe more*. More importantly, make a habit of learning from your previous mistakes, because not everyone knows that:

The lesson is repeated until it is learned.
Never forget this.

FIGHT FOR YOUR OWN IDEAS

"Your success will be determined by
your own confidence and fortitude."'
—Michelle Obama, former First Lady, author

Many parents, guardians, and relatives show their affection to younger generations through food and nice clothes. They look after their children and grandchildren by giving them all they need. This is how most parents behave regarding their little ones. There is just one teeny tiny problem. They overlook something that is even more important than food, shelter, and nice clothes: instilling children with the right mindset that would allow their boys and girls to gain a place in the world and be successful accordingly. Money can buy utilities, and can help in many other ways, but only attitude makes a difference at the end of the day. How you react in the face of life's everyday adversities and obstacles, and how you face a problem when it shows up and seems bigger than you, are key:

A winning attitude can do wonders.
A losing one will shove you right down
to the ground.

Money disappears quickly when placed in the wrong hands, yet many are unaware that money is just a means to increase what we already are and possess. Numerous are the cases of people who win the lottery or inherit great wealth, only to fork out everything shortly afterwards, returning to poverty once again. Why is that? Because if they were already spendthrifts beforehand, what happens is that when they win the money, all they do is turn into worse spendthrifts.

One of the biggest mistakes we unconsciously make is to constantly talk negatively about ourselves and others. Deep down, we all have an inner monologue that works non-stop and formulates thousands of thoughts every day. Unfortunately, we cannot shut down that inner voice inside us. Like Jiminy, the talking cricket in the Walt Disney classic, *Pinocchio©*, it never stops having its say in everything we do and say. Result? The voice conditions us for good and for bad in whatever we do. A problem arises when that little voice fills us up with pessimism and negativity. This is when we unconsciously sabotage ourselves in whatever we would like to perform so badly, but we fail! After all, who would commit to anything if an inner voice repeatedly told them it is not worth it? That we will be losing from the start? That we are terrible? That this will be just another fiasco?

Most parents and guardians provide all manner of comforts to their little ones out of affection, but neglect to provide a winning mindset that stands up to the world and its numerous challenges. We have already mentioned this. Tony was the same. Anytime I went against his will, he would do his best to scold me in an attempt to make me follow his way of thinking; no weird stuff for him, like going on an adventure around the world. I have already spoken about travelling, but it is worth stressing this point once more. Reluctance to travel is indicative of a reluctance to exit one's comfort zones, because it never gives us the opportunity to challenge our ideas, culture, and mindset, among other things. It's not surprising that Tony grew up so small-minded. Too accustomed to living in the same spot, surrounded by the same people, he would not tolerate this extravagant idea of wasting time and money to go somewhere for a prolonged period of time. By contrast, Mary thought otherwise. Having travelled herself in her twenties, she always pushed me to discover the world, if I could. Thanks to her, this is how I went abroad after high school. Like the talking cricket mentioned above, she was the voice telling me what to do for my own sake.

Other than travelling, there was another thing about which my parents were totally at odds. My rich-minded mom had a winning attitude. She would always believe in her own ideas, and fight for them. Usually, those who get started and show constancy along the way are typically also the individuals that get the biggest share. How? Because not only do they take their own share, but also that of all those who dropped out along the way. The same happens for e-commerce and the Internet as a whole. Many enthusiastically throw themselves into this project or that idea, but very few really hold on to it. And guess who makes the real money: those who have original ideas, no matter how extravagant they may be. They are those who are determined enough to persist when things take a bad turn, and who, despite all manner of obstacles and downfalls, give it one more try, and one more try, until they get the results they expected. Making mistakes is normal. We all make some due to inexperience. What is key is not to get discouraged when experiencing them. Rather, standing one's ground, and making all of the necessary corrections to optimize one's initial strategies. This is called experience. It allows one to sharpen the saw and make real progress over time. More importantly, successful people have a *winning formula*:

1) They don't doubt their skills.
2) They don't allow anyone to shake them and put them off.
3) They show a winning attitude all the way through.

I have a question for you: how can you possibly attract investors if you, for one, don't believe in your own ideas? People buy certainty. They want enthusiasm. That said, you have to firmly believe in it first. In fact, if you don't show that hyper-confidence, someone that should invest in you will certainly spot your uncertainty in your voice and attitude. Result? They won't jeopardize their money for someone who doesn't fully believe themselves and their strategies and methods first. It creates this domino effect and it all starts with you being in the front line. If you make the first move, a chain reaction occurs. By contrast, if you stay put, all the rest will remain still. No wonder so many stagnate. If they stay where they are with what they already have, that's all they get.

Tony was a case in point. He would think of all the scenarios that could go wrong. Also, when things were taking a bad turn, he would quickly give up and change his mind, turning his attention to something easier. Now, changing quickly, being flexible, and keeping up with the times can be seen as a plus in most companies, but this was not Tony's case. He simply lacked self-confidence to persist in any project he had his eyes on. As such, at the very first obstacle or failed attempt, he would promptly change, turning his attention to something less risky.

By contrast, Mary was more the type to try again and again, if it was something she was really into. Luckily, she passed this trait of hers on to me. She taught me to be persistent in whatever I believed in, and to make a project and stick with it, regardless of how challenging it may be.

If you take a look at butterflies, they never stay for long on one particular flower. They change every so often, on the lookout for new pollen. That said, don't behave like a butterfly. Because:

> **If you have an idea, and believe in it,**
> **no matter how foolish it may be,**
> **you should not give it up easily.**

This is a world filled with people who are champions at judging and criticizing others. It is curious that so many spend their own lives focusing on others, rather than on their own flaws and blind spots. Gossip is a perfect example; it shows how much we waste our time, focus and energy on others, rather than on ourselves. As Paulo Coelho reminds us, "Everyone seems to have a clear idea of how other people should lead their lives, but none about his or her own."[7]

This is a clear reminder that we should give more attention to ourselves, rather than to others. This is not selfish, believe me. If anything, it is about getting to know yourself better. Only then are you likely to know who you really are and what you really want. This is worth repeating: Only then are you likely to know who you really are and what you really want.

Being too focused on others leads us to forget about ourselves, let alone our goals and projects. As for these, they all start out as ideas in the mind. Every great invention started out as a plain idea, even weird ones – the electric bulb by Thomas Edison, the television by John Logie Baird, or the calculator by Blaise Pascal. The same applies for the printing press, the cinema, the automobile, and so on. Even nowadays, in the age of social networks and globalization, many have made large fortunes from random ideas. They may have seemed random at first, but blended with perseverance, and some tweaking here and there, their inventions went far. This is what happened with Amazon®. Slowly but surely, by surmounting all manner of obstacles and having full faith, it became the giant we all know today. The same goes for Alibaba®. There are myriad examples, but the logic remains the same. They all have a common denominator called *perseverance* in whatever they are into, although, it must be pointed out that they fought for their own ideas, as well. They had to have faith when no one believed in them, or worse, when they were laughed at. They had a strong faith, indeed, in order not to let obstacles, naysayers, or doubters detour them. The Wright brothers, for example, had only a little budget, no media attention, and sceptical people all around them. Nonetheless, they kept it going, and the rest is history. Regardless of money, a strong *Why* was at the root of it all. I ignore whether or not they had rich- or poor-minded parents in this instance. All I know is that scepticism and negativity are so widespread that no wonder so many become easily influenced by these two deadly factors; they are deadly because they kill ideas, and without ideas, nothing comes out of the hat.

So dear reader, remember to fight for your own ideas. Don't let poor-minded parents or relatives get in the way and take you off track. Sure, what's in your mind may sound bizarre, or weird to them. Even so, don't throw in the towel. If you do, nothing will spring up from your garden of ideas. As weak seeds don't grow into anything, neither do passing ideas. They don't bloom on their own unless someone constantly waters them with energy and dedication. In fact, the best fertilizers you can use are your determination and perseverance. Sure, you may be forced to change your strategy or tweak your initial plans due to external factors. No one has perfect plans, me included. By taking steps, one at a time, good things will certainly spring out from your ground of constancy.

I, for one, am not the kind of person to take all the credit myself. A great contribution of my ideas comes from Mary. In a person's prime, it is normal to ask for help and guidance, and I was no exception. Like everyone, I was also influenced in large part by the people I was spending most time with, especially at home. This means that without Mary's rich-minded advice, many of the things I had in my young mind, including plans and dreams for the future, would have never reached a tangible form without support. Of course, constancy was my job, but the initial boost to keep it going came from Mary. Unlike Tony, who would be the give-it-a-try type, only to change route when things took a nasty turn, Mary was the other way round. She would rather not be like a butterfly that easily flies from one flower to another. Instead, she would stick to one if she thought it was worth it. So I grew up with the same attitude as her. I strongly believed, for instance, that foreign languages would be an integral part of my future, and so it happened. I believed that a little action is preferable to one thousand nice words. I also believed that doing a job related to my studies was possible – not a mere privilege for a few chosen ones, but a right to all those who strongly believe in themselves and fight for their own ideas.

This is not the case for those who easily change according to circumstances and go where the wind blows. Sadly, this is what a great many people do. They see a profitable sector, a new tendency, a trend, and jump on the bandwagon, thinking they will make good money without breaking a sweat. Trading online and Bitcoin are just a few examples. Does it not seem strange that, all of a sudden, especially on social media, so many courses and gurus spring up like mushrooms, promising a luxury lifestyle, big cars, and working from the beach? That's not fighting for one's ideas; it is throwing smoke in people's eyes. The same goes for all those who play the lottery or gamble, hoping to become rich overnight, not understanding that all they are doing is throwing money away.

Usually, when a person fights for their own ideas, whether profitable or not, he or she would not behave like a butterfly, or pray to the sky. They may adjust their strategies, yes, but they keep the basis of the original plan or idea. That means staying put, despite the difficulties. Sure, this requires determination, but not having blinders over your eyes. I would recommend keeping a close eye on one's strategy and modifying it anytime it is necessary. But core ideas should remain the same throughout. The Bible, for example, has always had the same core values and beliefs. It didn't change roots through history to follow the tendencies of the moment.

So remember to learn from all of your previous mistakes. Second, firmly believe in your own ideas, regardless of what your peers or relatives may think. In the case they should criticize you, remind yourself that it is your life, not theirs. As such, feel free to do as you like:

> **Miracles occur to those who are tenacious.**
> **May you be that person one day.**

Be a rich-minded person (and parent) yourself:

Fight for your own ideas. Be a strong believer in what you are doing. Be determined, but avoid stubbornness. Change your approach when something is not taking you anywhere, and don't be a perfectionist. Be flexibly minded in case the circumstances require doing so. And please, don't think you can do everything on your own. Drop this egocentric idea of being independent at all costs. It can only cause a burnout in the long run. That said, don't be blind like Tony because of your pride. If you are, you may stumble many times, wasting time, money, and more importantly, your self-esteem. This usually happens when a person deems their strategy a winning one, while instead it may be so to their eyes only. Acknowledge your determination, but also your gaps in the fields that are unfamiliar to you. Ask for help, if necessary, especially if someone is more knowledgeable than you are. Lots of people are willing to help out, as long as you ask for it first.

SCARCITY THINKING

"You can overcome any obstacle.
You can achieve the most tremendous
things by faith power."
—**Norman Vincent Peale, preacher, author**

Taking care of ourselves is something we should all aim to do. Only through nurturing the body, mind and soul can we stand a chance of elevating ourselves. The same holds true for values, such as ethics, dignity, and a kind heart. This may appear obvious – even banal to some. Yet, it is not. Individuals may say they take care of themselves by going to the gym or by eating healthily, but quite frankly, that's not enough. What they disregard is to care for their own minds.

On a daily basis, too many of us have negative thoughts and pessimistic perspectives based on our past experiences. Because of that, we tend to see the half-empty glass pretty much everywhere. And it is on this basis that we plan our decisions. This can mean poor choices made in fear, due to the lack of trust for the future or any current outer circumstances. The issue is that when ruled by fear, we can make no big decision in our best interest. That is, we would rather take a step back than forward. And guess what? This is exactly how we miss countless opportunities throughout life, the same that then turn into regrets.

The Bible frequently talks about life's abundance. It says there is no such thing as scarcity. Yet this is what we see and perceive all around us; there is a lack of this and absence of that; there is scarcity of jobs, lack of money, and shortness of opportunities. When we hear colleagues or friends coming up with statements like, "Better safe than sorry," or, "Be careful what you wish for," or, "You can't be too careful," rarely will they come up with something powerful enough for a breakthrough. Certainly, they say these things for their own security, but safety and success hardly live together, if at all. Where one dwells, the other cannot thrive, and vice versa.

Life is full of twists, turns, obstacles, and detours. We know that all too well, but it is not all doom and gloom. The problem is, our minds are so accustomed to reasoning this way that we see the bad before anything else, and the negative stands out over the good in most cases. Not by chance, insurance firms make tons of money out of this. The possibility of damage is so strong, in our minds most of all, that it means those companies rake in the dollars. Governments and banks use the same scaremongering tactics. Since ancient times, fear has been used to control the masses, to make them do whatever powerful entities had in mind. In fact, when fear is central, people instinctively look for protection, and this makes them more and more inclined to obey the establishment.

If life is meant to be "abundant" as the Bible states on many occasions, why then is there so much widespread depression, fear, and sadness? Why are we so afraid of getting deprived of the little we own? And why are we under the impression that we cannot obtain what we wish for? As said above, the problem is scarcity, or to put in better terms, *scarcity-thinking*. It is not your fault, though. You were raised to think that way, putting into practice what you were taught at a tender age. Because the majority of us grew up as scarcity thinkers, we see a lack of this and shortness of that anytime, anywhere. Due to this, people prefer to "play it safe." To them, words like *abundance* and *wealth* are pie-in-the-sky. They fail to see beyond the surface, not due to a lack of brains, but because they haven't trained their minds to see beyond what is visible. So accustomed to spotting and choosing what is easy, they disregard asking themselves if it is the right thing to do. Usually, what's right tends to be more challenging and far less pleasant. It goes without saying that an individual with an easy-to-get-stuff-done approach will likely avoid that route. Rather, he or she would opt for the easy path for the simple reason that it is easy, ignoring the time, patience, and effort that the right thing would require to get to new heights. As a side note, rarely is what's right on par with simplicity. Taking this into account, the majority still do not want to do whatever it takes to achieve more lasting and satisfactory goals. Next time you are undecided about which route to take, bear in mind that:

Abundance is (and has always been)
at the mercy of everyone.
You just need to learn to spot it.

"How do I spot what is right for me?" you may legitimately ask.

First of all, by changing your thought patterns and perspective on what your upbringing taught you. People don't often see what is *right* because they were raised to mainly spot what is handy and risk-free, not recognizing hidden opportunities. And if parents lacked this ability, guess what? Children are very likely to be brought up in the same way. Let's not forget that we are the by-product of all of our previous experiences, and an integral part among those past experiences is our family's teachings.

So used to seeing what is at our fingertips, many tend to reject all the rest, that is, the hard and time-consuming stuff. Well, the magic does not happen within the comfort zone, in case you didn't know. Just step out of it and see what happens: routine disappears and boredom fades away, because ease and excitement do not go hand in hand. If anything, simplicity goes together with routine and boredom, whereas magic goes along with uncomfortableness and uneasiness. The same holds true for opportunities. These can only be spotted by a trained mind. If you have trained yours to see the good and not just the bad, as well as potential, hidden possibilities, you are more likely to perceive them when they are before you. You won't just pass by the possibilities, because while it is a habit for the untrained mind to disregard them, it is also a habit for the trained mind to spot one when it is close by.

You can be sure that a scarcity thinker would not see an opportunity even if it was right under their nose. Too busy whining and complaining about how hard and unfair life is, he or she would just get passed by, as if nothing happened. Do not feel sorry for them. They are the ones at fault. Opting for comforts and shortcuts is always a matter of choice, a lifestyle, a way of living, not a condemnation from the sky. Not coincidentally, luck hardly ever knocks on the doors of these people. Opportunities are rarely lying on the easy path. Rather, they are more likely to sit on the less beaten track, the same most people intentionally avoid out of fear. Metaphorically speaking, scarcity thinking can be seen as a virus slowing down your internal software. The outcome? Living within the minimum of our possibilities, throwing away the one life that we possess over an existence of routine and dissatisfaction.

Mistakenly, we think we are short of everything, starting with luck. Likewise, we listen to naysayers – oftentimes coming from within the domestic walls – and take to heart whatever they say. This is how their trash becomes our trash too. This is how scarcity thinking and old mindsets pass from the elders to the young. We live below our potential, in a never-ending state of constant struggle to stay afloat due to this passage of bad thinking from older to newer generations. This is how we inherit this misconception of always being at a loss. This convinces us that we must make it through life, accepting a job we don't like, buying things we cannot afford, or accepting that others will decide for us.

My father was a champion of scarcity thinking who always settled for less and found some sort of compromise just to have something in the bag. In a previous chapter, we went through fighting for your own ideas. This implies avoiding settling for less and underestimating your real value. Hospitality is a case in point. When I lived in the UK, being a waiter or barman meant being paid the minimum wage. Now, I have met many good waiting staff, and one of their common complaints was their pay. Both good and average waiters were paid the same, regardless of commitment, passion, and effort. Was it fair? Of course not. How can a professional waiter or barman be paid the same as a mediocre, or inexperienced colleague? This is why it is fundamental to believe in your value and to fight to have it recognized. You must make a point that you are worth more than what you may be offered during an interview. It is not unusual for many working environments to have skilled staff that earn way too little with regard to their expertise. So, next time someone offers you less than you think you deserve, remember this:

> ***Do not settle for less.***
> ***If you do, you underestimate yourself,***
> ***and over time you will accept that***
> ***you are actually worth less than you are.***

To apply this, you must be the first to be convinced of your real worth. If you are, the way you behave and speak will make you sound more convincing in this regard, and eventually others will believe in you, too. However, if you are the first to doubt yourself, others will follow. As seen in the hospitality example above, others will decide how much you and your time are worth, but because you are worthy (believe me, you are), you deserve to step up and evolve. You deserve to be more and become more of what you are right now. Life can give you much more than what it is giving you at the moment, if you let it.

Beliefs work miracles. It is strong faith that moves mountains and sets us in motion through an internal boost called *determination*. By contrast, scepticism won't give you the same push. Note: this is the same boost that you need so badly to get yourself out of mediocrity, in terms of relationships, work, and friends, but of course, you won't be able to change your family's nature. Unfortunately, that is one of the few things you can't modify at will. However, you can always set the tone and be the one to lead the way. How? By being an example of optimism, courage, and determination. In doing so, over time you are more likely to positively influence those around you with your good actions and positive energy.

While this rings true for adults, young children cannot do this for obvious reasons. It is then the parents' duty to set the pace for them by setting the standards of a correct, dignified way of living and way of thinking that is not just average. This is because if the former are raised to think that life is difficult and unfair, where one must always settle for less, how do you think the children's mindset will end up? Exactly. They will accept whatever is around them, and risk opportunists taking advantage of them. Unfortunately, what may be within reach is not always in line with our ambitions. Sad, but true. This is why you need to fight for yourself, without ever thinking scarcity. No one will do it for you. Only you and you alone can do this. It won't be easy, but all successful people excel not because they are lucky, or rich, or recommended by some prominent friends, but because after stumbling countless times, they got up, learned their lesson, and tried one more time, and one more time, until they eventually pulled it off.

It is not opportunities that are scarce, like Tony always thought and tried to teach me. We all hit some snags from time to time. It's just that we simply aren't able to spot them when they present themselves before us. In case you are part of this group, ask yourself: "Is my mind trained to spot opportunities when they present themselves before me?" If not, it is likely that you were brought up by scarcity thinkers, are now a scarcity thinker yourself, and over time their view has unconsciously become your own:

A negative and scarce mind won't see the positives, even when they are in plain sight.

Too focused to foresee any potential trouble, scarcity thinkers prefer to stay where they are with what is already available to them. Too afraid to venture out in some uncharted territory, all too many prefer to stay within their comfort zones, in the company of other scarcity thinkers. As they put it, *misery loves company*. You should steer clear of such company, made up of complaining and non-stop whining. Why? Because they can so easily influence you in a negative way. These are typically the same individuals who, at the end of every year, pray for a better one, hoping for a miracle from the sky. The issue is that they just pray, but don't do what it really takes to get to their goal: *action*. By contrast, if you stay in the company of abundance thinkers, the conversation will be very different. They won't talk about cheap gossip, their neighbors, or how bad their jobs are. If anything, ideas would be the prime subject, and they won't say you can't do this or achieve that. Instead, they will encourage you to risk it, and plan to get where you want to go. Successful people, unlike Tony-style folks, won't tell you to hang your head, or settle for less. They will teach you to reason on your own two feet:

If you think life is hard or unfair, before blaming God, ask yourself: Were my previous decisions made wisely?

The funny thing is that scarcity thinkers not only avoid risks like the plague, but they also spend endless time complaining because nothing ever changes in their lives. They complain of feeling stuck in their ruts and feel helpless as a result. When we are little, we are like sponges soaking up whatever is around us. As we know nothing about life in our early years, we take in all of our parents' and grandparents' teachings. In doing so, their vision of the world becomes our vision, too. If they don't like a certain food, for example, we are likely to grow up believing that such food is bad. And not just food. We are taught not to talk to strangers, to go to bed early, to say please when asking for something, and so on. This is how their teachings become our own *Commandments*. Our parents being our first teachers, we (the children) willingly welcome whatever they say without reservation. So, if they teach youngsters to avoid risks, to be happy as they are, and that dangers are always around the corner, how will those youngsters eventually grow up? They will grow up to stay in a box, a little damned box for the rest of their lives.

To go back to scarcity thinking, if we were brought up to settle for less, to be content as we are, and to accept whatever is around us, how will our mindset be later on? How will we grow up as a teenager and then as an adult? To settle for less, of course. To avoid risks, and to stay in our little world, having less than we deserve. I will tell you something, dear reader, *you don't have to end up this way*. If you were taught poorly, you can always bounce back and start over again. Incidentally, be sure to treasure the summaries at the end of each chapter. They are there for you, to make you become a better you. Also, in case you already have children, or plan to have some anytime soon, make a point of being the parent you wish you'd had. It is never too late.

Be a rich-minded person (and parent) yourself:

If it is true that life starts at the end of the comfort zone, why steer clear from it out of fear? We may have been taught this in our prime, but no one is forcing us to continue down any road. That said, if you don't like your current situation, built up from numerous past mistakes, wrong decisions, and bad teachings, do yourself a favor: change right now! No one will do it for you, that's for sure. You and you alone can change, especially if who you are and what you are experiencing at the minute are not very satisfactory. If you were raised by someone like Tony to settle for less, start believing in yourself and your capabilities more often. Do not accept whatever is around you just to avoid being empty-handed. Not every mushroom in the woods is good for your health. Open yourself up to the new, but be selective in whatever is offered to you. Do so, and the world will appear to be at your feet, more abundant and generous than ever before. If you are sceptical, just give it a go. You have nothing to lose.

THINKING ON YOUR FEET

"The one who follows the crowd will usually get no further than the crowd.
The one who walks alone, is likely to find himself in places
no one has ever been."
—Albert Einstein, theoretical physicist,
developer of the theory of relativity

We are known to be social animals. Deep down, we have a strong desire to bond and fit in, particularly with those with whom we share common traits. This is how communities get created, both online and in-person. These are formed in order to share ideas and experiences of any kind. Again, we do this because we have a natural tendency to fit in with groups, communities, clubs, you name it. Especially in the advent of social media, more and more relationships are being formed online every day. This is all fine and well, if it wasn't for one problem: a great deal of people, notably among the young, do very foolish things in order to be accepted into these so-called groups, communities, and clubs. Dressing inappropriately, smoking, binge drinking, and other such things can be employed for this social climb. Showing off and appearing trendy can be mistaken as a trademark of courage and value. They crave social acceptance and admiration from their peers, both on the Internet and in real life.

As anticipated, this longing makes us do the most absurd things. Nowadays, more and more teens do nonsensical acts, taking on even risky feats just to be in the spotlight. While in the past being the center of attention meant to be applauded, now it is all down to how many likes and comments one collects. Judging the cleverness of an uploaded video is not the point here. Rather, we should question its roots. Why do we do what we do? What pushes a teen to jump off a high cliff, or cross over a train track with their camera on?

Becoming a celebrity for stupid deeds is very easy. Becoming popular for something clever is way harder.

Becoming famous for careless acts is so damn easy and quick nowadays. Acts like throwing cakes or rocks at the *Mona Lisa*, dyeing Rome's Trevi fountain red, drinking a whole bottle of spirits and then going swimming, and many others, are so common now that we don't get surprised at them anymore. It is no shock to hear the culprit saying they did what they did for a moment of popularity. Well, while becoming popular for a marathon or a special award is quite something, being cited in the news for robbery or bullying is a different story. They both make headlines, true, but one is admirable and remarkable, while the other is shameful and idiotic. Why is it so recurrent to hear about negative stuff making the front page?

There are several reasons. For certain, it is easier and less time-consuming to get spotted that way. This makes it the preferred route. Another reason is that this society of instant gratification makes us impatient, very impatient, indeed. All of this is to the detriment of real, long-term achievements – those that would leave an indelible mark behind. Well, it took the Wright brothers years before taking flight. It took Virginia Woolf more than a decade to become a well-known writer and feminist, and it took Jeff Bezos even longer before putting in place the online platform we all know. Patience blended with constancy are critical to creating something worthy of ourselves and, more importantly, history. The quick, easy, dopamine-releasing stints of pleasure are not. Rather, acts that require blood, sweat, and tears are more likely to make an impact.

Society has wrongly taught us that waiting is bad, and that everything is fast-paced and in constant evolution. As a result, we can't help but keep up. The only issue with this is that speed does not allow us to pause and reflect. It does not give us the time to stop and see the process. Instead, we try to be ever faster in order to keep the pace, grasp opportunities, and beat the competition. This is just a big illusion, if you ask me. When quality is at stake, revision and double-checking require time, and often plenty of it. Rarely is it possible to deliver high-quality products or services without double- or triple-checking one's job first. When aiming high, it is usually the details that make a difference. This also holds true for competition, but even if you are not competing, you won't go the extra mile if you are rushing it all the time.

You see, speed is pointless if you neglect to reinforce the basics, and nothing solid can be built upon weak foundations:

Strong basics and continuous revision are critical if you want to go places.

Believe it or not, both checking and revising require time. There is no alternative. As author Stephen Covey puts it in his book, *The Seven Habits of Highly Successful People*, one of the pillars of success lies in "sharpening the saw."[8] This is to strengthen what you already know before branching out on something new, becoming ever stronger and better by continual self-renewal. We must spend time reinforcing what we already know, because only then can we branch out towards new things. Like a blade that needs constant sharpening to cut properly, you also need to revise what you already know before moving on to new areas or levels. This is how you can achieve excellence – which is different from perfection – in whatever field you set your sites on. I, for one, do not believe in perfection, as we are in continual, non-stop progression. I see it this way:

Achieving excellence and delivering high standards are very much feasible, as long as an individual takes the time to reinforce the basics.

Being fast-paced is an enemy to all this. In fact, it makes it almost impossible to focus enough on what we already know and master the subject. This is how we end having gaps of knowledge in pretty much everything. Because the masses behave by being fast and quick, now you know that this is not the best option for you. If you, too, don't want to have those gaps in your knowledge, take your time to brush up on your wisdom. Not only will this strengthen what you already know, but you will also gain more and more details as you go. By contrast, rushing it won't give you any spare time to check out how you are doing, never mind spotting any weak areas you may have in the moment.

We are first taught at home and later at school to jump on subjects we like. If we don't manage to, we are encouraged to move on to something else more suitable to our capacities. We have all gone through this. What parents and teachers substantially ignore is that success does not sit along the easy road. It sits on the road less travelled, because, if it was easy, everyone would be successful, wealthy and happy. It is less travelled (and thus less crowded) because it is more demanding per se. It is less frequented because many listened to their poor-minded parents and old-school teachers, learning to avoid the hassle of what's right, despite being more challenging in itself. The downside is that ease goes hand-in-hand with boredom and routine, leading to the average as a result. Conversely, opting for the difficult, less popular options may be more traumatic, due to their demanding nature. The good news is, once they click in and familiarize themselves with the option, they won't experience boredom and monotony anymore; that's guaranteed. They will experience excitement for being in new and uncharted territories, and fulfilment will follow for achieving new heights.

Like society, my poor-minded father tried to convince me that because something has never been done before, it cannot be done at all. He recommended that I don't stray far from the safe route, where everything is visible and predictable. Now, to the majority of us, risking it may not sound nice by itself, but let me ask you a simple question: since when are great things delivered on a silver platter? Very few are! Since when is the unexpected or the unknown easy to obtain? Not very often. Inventors could not really benchmark the best in class, as there was no one to copy from. All they did was to give it a shot, making countless corrections until they got it right. Leonardo da Vinci was a great observer of birds, and from that he wrote and planned some of his best creations. He knew humans were too heavy to take flight. Yet, he didn't give up on his idea, despite knowing humans are not meant for it. He followed through and designed his own flying machine. If he had listened to the naysayers, doubters and downers (including family, friends, neighbors, and colleagues), he would soon have been forgotten after his death. Consider this:

**You may not have the money to start out,
but that is not what counts.
What matters most is that you have a strong purpose.
Once you have a strong "Why,"
the "How" generally finds its way through.**

Tony has always had a weak "Why". That's the reason he was giving up very easily on pretty much anything demanding. Anytime a task turned out to be too challenging, he would take a different route, or cut corners. He behaved in this manner because he was taught so from school and his own parents many years before, and that's how he wanted to bring me up, too.

You can see for yourself how damaging it can be to have poor-minded parents. Countless are the boys and girls who grow up with the same minds as their parents, who are taught to hang their heads and opt for the easy, less demanding road. It all starts out in our prime, from the people with whom we spend most time: our parents.

If this may shake you as you go back in time in your mind right now, be mindful of this: *you cannot change your past.* What is done is done. Period. But you can always be accountable for today. How? By becoming a rich-minded person now, and a rich-minded parent later on, if you wish. Give yourself and your children a winning mindset. This is absolutely feasible if you make it a priority, especially if your children (current or future ones) are still under your wing.

I am saying this because the world is filled with gifted people – super smart boys and girls working for ordinary wages. These are people settling for less while they could be making a fortune, if only they were bold enough to exploit their talents, avoiding selling themselves short.

Numberless are the people with good intentions, but as Mahatma Gandhi put it, "You must be the change you wish to see in the world."[9] This means that, to change the world, you must first change yourself. The first step to it is reason with your own head, rather than to merely flock with the others. In addition to this, Albert Einstein reminds us that there is always a price to pay for being like the others. He stated, "The one who follows the crowd will usually get no further than the crowd."[10] Simply put, by following your peers, you can't help but obtain the same results as them. You may play it safe this way, yes, but that won't make you go places. That's for sure.

A few examples? I have always been critical about fashion. Current trends among teens, for instance, are wearing torn jeans and having tattoos. Some may say I am old-fashioned, but I prefer to go through everything in a critical way. To me, torn jeans make no sense, for the simple reason that they leave parts uncovered and, in the event of cold, this can create ligament issues in the long run. The same goes for tattoos. A trend is temporary and so are personal tastes. By contrast, tattoos last a lifetime. No surprise then that so many turn to surgery to get them removed after a while. Isn't it strange to spend money to have something inscribed on your body, and then to pay again to have it removed a few years later? I am sorry to say this, but trends are just one of the many everyday examples of people behaving like herd animals. The leader promotes something, and the masses obey without question. An icon, or idol, or VIP wears a specific piece of clothing – usually paid by companies for doing so – and what do their fans do? They follow blindly without reservation; without considering whether they really like it or not.

I will never tire of saying this: be critical, especially when it comes to adopting new behaviors or habits. Reason with your own head and process everything before making it your own. So many people adopt foolish behaviors every day but didn't give it proper thought first. Are you afraid you won't be socially accepted by your peers if you do? Are you afraid of becoming an outcast of sorts? Well, if a person is nice, those nearby will notice it. Similarly, if one is dishonest or a born liar, he or she may be the coolest dude in the room but, sooner or later, people will avoid him or her. I personally think that:

Those who are kind and fair-hearted will never be truly alone.

You don't need to follow the masses to prove yourself. Behave naturally. Follow ethics and be a person of morals. Be good, and most likely similar people will be attracted to you. You don't need to wear a mask or fake your actions to appear cool or up to someone else's expectations. You can still be fascinating by setting a good example as a healthy, good old role model to others.

Be a rich-minded person (and parent) yourself:

If you want to go far, don't be a herd animal. If the common way is to find any job, earn some money, and settle down until retirement, like Tony did, have the guts to disagree. Follow in someone else's footsteps instead. There are countless examples of individuals who dropped out of university or college, making their fortunes somewhere else. Be a critical thinker and analyze what is around you before making it yours. This is usually how others' garbage becomes our garbage. Nope, use your intelligence and look out for great ideas and winning behaviors. Only then can you make them part of you. Make a point of asking yourself more often, "Will I become a better person by adopting this new behavior or habit?" If the answer is yes, then go for it. If not, look for another route. Just remember that there is always an alternative route, choice, and plan for those who make the time to look for one.

THE IMPORTANCE OF GIVING

"The best way to find yourself is
to lose yourself in the service of others."
—**Mahatma Gandhi, political ethicist, proponent of nonviolence**
for freedom of India

In a world where nothing is done for free, we need to learn to give. We need to be givers rather than mere takers. Speaking like this may sound weird, even abnormal, especially in a society where money rules, and nothing is done for free. It is true that there are many steadfast charities helping thousands of people every day, but those are an exception. In everyday life, no one does anything unless there is something to gain from it.

No one can deny that we live in an age of enlightenment and mass technology. Despite this so-called enlightenment, we have become so afraid of anything we can't see, touch, and measure that we fear whatever is beyond our reach and cannot be controlled. Similarly, we are so scared of the idea of taking risks that we prefer to step backwards rather than forwards. Taking all of this into account, it is fair to point out:

No one ever made real money,
or huge rewards by playing it safe.

Two questions arise here: how can we be creative if we want guarantees all the time? How can we be sure in advance that our efforts will pay off?

With a paid job, it's possible, because you exchange your time for a safe paycheck. Being self-employed, by contrast, does not provide the same level of certainty. Self-employed people take risks, sometimes huge ones, but it is usually these people who eventually make the real money and, in many cases, become millionaires:

***It is usually the leader, not the followers,
that makes a fortune.***

Still, the vast majority crave guarantees. This is why they happily trade their time for money. This brings about the fact that not only must they follow others' rules, but also they are not really allowed to be creative. How can one be expressive if they need to follow someone else's guidelines and protocols all the time? In a similar manner, traditional schooling has always discouraged creativity. As it is, the educational system trains people to follow the rules – to become good employees. It does not teach us to turn into employers, nor to create jobs or make money. Rather, it instructs us to be "good soldiers" and obey the rules without question.

Speaking of guarantees, let's ask ourselves: did Thomas Edison asked for guarantees when he was working on an invention? Did he demand success right away before even getting started? Of course not. He got himself and his team up and running and made all the necessary changes along the way.

In fact, when trying out something for the first time, you cannot copy or base your ideas on someone else's work. You have no one from whom to draw inspiration or to model. This is when you can give creativity unlimited space and form. This is the time in which you can do whatever your brain or your instinct tell you, allowing you to reach new heights that you never thought you would reach. In the absence of guidelines or rules, failure levels are certainly high – very high, indeed. In fact, Edison and his team made thousands of attempts before creating something revolutionary. They didn't just create the light bulb, but also the phonograph, and the carbon transmitter, among other inventions. It didn't happen overnight, of course; it took thousands and thousands of attempts to reach something worthy of note. Had Edison given up easily on his work, as do many of our peers nowadays, our lives could be quite different now. That was an extreme example, but the bottom-line is: YOU HAVE TO TAKE RISKS TO HAVE A LIFE WORTH LIVING. In addition:

***Taking risks gives you
a higher chance of success.***

The same goes with giving first, without necessarily expecting something back. Most of us are so scared by the mere thought of being taken advantage of, or ripped off, that we want to see upfront what we will receive in return for our time, actions, and generosity. There is no denying that the world as we know it is laden with both opportunists and cheats. Fortunately, they are a minority. The majority are honest people who are willing to help, return favors, and assist whenever possible, provided that you ask for assistance first.

Likewise, a few pieces of litter in the streets do not make the whole population uncivilized. If a man harasses a woman, that does not make all males bad. A few bad apples do not make the whole world a bad place in which to live. This sounds obvious, yet, it is not. Why? Because when it comes to taking risks, the majority get defensive, sceptical, and trust nobody. They say, "Because of negative experiences in the past, I want guarantees," or, "I won't lift a finger without something in writing beforehand." This is how the world runs nowadays; everything must be on paper, signed, and with a stamp on it. This is how most of the population thinks and behaves. How to prove them wrong? No one likes a rip-off, nor do they want to lose money or be taken advantage of, but the whole world isn't made up of parasites.

The problem here is that due to a narrow-minded approach, we tend to generalize all the time. If one thing is bad, then everything might be bad, too. Being doubtful of whoever stands before us, we are not willing to take a risk, especially when our money is at stake. And here we go again. It is not by chance that the world is getting more selfish, greedy, and detached. There is too much suspicion and zero trust, unless money or papers talk first.

My rich-minded mother was the type of person who would trust people based on their good will. Unfortunately, this was the very reason she got cheated many times. Not everyone is a saint. Nonetheless, she decided – courageously, I would add – to remain a trusting person. She continued to be caring and to believe in others' good consciences, and trusted people based on their word without the need for a binding contract. To her, agreements or promises were verbal, as she tended to trust – a noble behavior, but not one that was risk-free. By contrast, poor-minded Tony, having also experienced scams in his younger years, was the type of person who would not believe a word without being shown a receipt, a signed paper, or anything else as a back-up. A completely different approach, but at least he was encountering fewer rip-offs in comparison to Mary. How can we blame him? No one likes to be used or taken advantage of, but how can we live a good life by being defensive and distrustful all the time? How happy can we be in living like that?

When I was very little, both of my parents used to give me money to buy groceries at the nearby store. There was a difference, however: Mary would give me the money and expect her goods in return, but she would trust my good will as far as the leftover change was concerned. Tony would do the same, but after sending me to the nearby shop, with counted money, he would demand the groceries, the change, and a receipt back. He needed to verify how much I had actually spent in order to ensure that I wouldn't keep any change. Even though I was his son, I still had to show a receipt and return the sum shown on the receipt. Fortunately for me, being aware of this conduct, my rich-minded mother would let me keep the change from time to time.

I am sure that you will have noticed a difference here. One is a giver, the other just a taker. A poor-minded person would mainly expect favors, and to *receive* from others. Most of us have surely met someone who is a scrounger, someone who habitually asks for small change, a cigarette, a lift, etc., without understanding that doing so incessantly is just so wrong. It demonstrates a lack of respect to all the good-hearted people who are unable to say NO. The same holds true for those in a position of command, like managers and employers. At previous hotels or restaurants where I worked, managers usually expected favors from their staff. To them, it was second nature that because they provided work, they could do whatever they wanted with their staff and their time. Now, I am usually a generous and available person, but I did notice when a superior was taking advantage of their staff. Unfortunately, this wasn't just the case for the hospitality industry. As far as I could see, takers never seemed to be satiated when it came to receiving and having people at their service.

If we think it over, this occurs everywhere, all the time. People are not really used to being the first to give because they have this inner fear of not getting paid back. As for the few who are willing to be the first to give, they are easily spotted and targeted by opportunists at the earliest convenience. Due to this risk, what should we do at this point? How can we be generous and available without the hassle of being ripped off? According to Norman

Vincent Peale, "The secret of the law of abundance is this: in order to receive and appreciate the good things of life, you must first give."[11]

In case you are not familiar with the Law of Abundance, the premise is that whatever you are willing to give to the world will come back to you multiplied in unexpected ways. So, be a generous person and you will be rewarded abundantly for doing so.

My advice is to make others aware that you are available. Essentially, aim to give first and be a caring person like Mary was. I would suggest, though, keeping your eyes peeled when being altruistic. This means that if you do someone a favor, or help out when someone is in need, check if they are willing to return the favor at a later date.

When life gets too hectic, we can't help but ask for help, but we also need to bear in mind that we must be grateful and give something back from time to time. If you made yourself available to a friend or colleague of yours, are they now willing to return the favor when you need a helping hand? If the answer is yes, you did well to help out. If they come up with excuses, once, twice, three times, you should still be happy for your previous good actions. As stated above, to an opportunist, whatever they receive will never be enough; they will always ask for more. Eventually they will also end up alone for doing so. By contrast, altruistic people like yourself will always have some friends to count on.

Be a rich-minded person (and parent) yourself:

If you are a giver, you will never be lonely. More importantly, people will think and speak well of you, both in your presence and behind your back. It is so damn easy to be remembered for good deeds, but it is even easier to be remembered for bad actions. Be a giver like Mary, and you won't ever be left alone. Stay alert for opportunists though, as it is so shamefully in their nature to always ask, without ever returning favors. To them, your assistance, money, and time will never be enough, because once they learn how kind-hearted you are, they will always come to you and ask for more. Unfortunately, the more you tend to give, the more they are willing to expect. Luckily, they are but a minority. For those with good morals and a shred of ethics, be willing to give first, even if they are not able to return the favor straight away. Sooner or later, they will assist you in some way or other. Mary was one who always helped first. In return, she was never really alone. She could always count on her son's assistance, or that of relatives, especially when she got divorced and needed moral support and economic assistance. This is, indeed, what makes people *rich* – not the size of their wallets or the speed of their phones. It is altruism. Think of those who are less fortunate. Be kind and generous to them, even if they are not able to repay you at the moment. You won't regret it.

DIGNITY AND ETHICS

"A man without ethics is a
wild beast loosed upon this world."
—Albert Camus, French philosopher, author,
1957 winner of Nobel Peace Prize in literature

There are some things in life that should never be questioned, traded, or put aside for temporary convenience. I am referring to personal values. These can be very subjective according to this or that person, but luckily there are a few values that are common to almost all of us: love, family, respect, friendship, ethics, and dignity. While all those are unquestionably important, at least from my perspective, dignity and ethics are perhaps the most "sacred" ones, and for good reason.

Dignity and ethics push us to behave in a certain way and encourage us to be just and respectful, not only to ourselves, but also to others. Particularly, these two values can guide us toward becoming a better person, starting from within. This is only possible if we decide to listen to our inner voice. In fact, it is out of choice that we are guided by morals and ethics, and in case you didn't realize:

No one is born dishonest, a cheat, or a liar.
We choose to become so.

Regarding this statement, there are many reasons that people end up this way. One of them is personal convenience. For instance, by always getting, without ever giving first, you are likely to receive a lot in terms of personal favors and money. You will always be "covered," in some ways. But at what price? As previously mentioned, no one likes to be used, or taken for a ride. A person who exploits others is likely to get some personal gain, at least at first, but the same individual is likely to remain isolated later on. In other words, since actions speak louder than words, selfish conduct will always push people away and the opportunist is likely to remain in isolation.

Furthermore, it is no surprise that the preferred method of revenge is bad-mouthing. So, if someone feels they were cheated, or used in some way, it is likely they will cover the opportunist with mud. Lots of it, in fact. With the ascent of social media, and sites like TripAdvisor® and Glassdoor®, it is bloody easy and practical to voice one's feelings and speak up. So if someone behaves badly, there is a real possibility that many —internet users, most of all — will know about it. Of course, many reviews and comments are fake, especially online, but when you come across two, three, or four users labelling *that* specific person, business, service, hotel or restaurant with similar words, one is very likely to speculate that the comments are true. That being said, the Bible reminds us: *"Treat others as you want to be treated"* (Matthew 7:12; Luke 6:31).

We've heard about this and many other quotes in elementary school, but here is the thing, or maybe the paradoxes: why, then, do some people grow up as liars and cheats? And why do they adopt the habit of always asking without ever giving? Why do they become opportunistic at every convenience? Or even worse, why would they sell their soul to the highest bidder? It can usually be seen coming from a mile away when someone sells themselves to others, like a superior at work. How? By the way they interact, or the fake smiles they put on their faces. And why do they behave in this way? Again, it is just out of convenience and the certainty of upcoming results, be it a promotion, a raise, bonuses, and why not – even power. Power has always been seductive to human beings. Why do you think many people are willing to do anything for money? Because for many people, especially materialistic people, increased wealth is equivalent to major power. Religion talks about the love of money being the source of all evil. In some ways, this is true. Why, then, are we so tempted to pile up so much of it? Is it a hobby? Not really. It is all about power, at least in our post-modern society. The more bucks we accumulate, the more our status and social capital are enhanced. Sad, but very true.

To return to morals and ethics, when a culprit blames their crime on the infamous environment into which they were born, this can be true, but only in part. It is true because, deep down, it was the person's decision to adopt a certain behavior or lifestyle that prompted them to break the law. No one is a born liar, traitor, burglar, smuggler, or worse, a murderer. These are the final outputs of a number of bad choices and poor decisions made beforehand. To put it another way, these are the results of listening to the wrong people and their bad advice.

During our prime, parents are the people with whom we stay most in contact. Then, as we grow up, we spend more and more time with friends and acquaintances. Basically, it all starts out with our dads and moms. If they have a poor mindset, guess what? You are more likely to grow up with a poor mindset yourself. At a tender age, your cells and your brain are not fully formed. It is called "tender age" for a reason; when we come into this world, we generally spend our first years absorbing our surroundings like a sponge. Our surroundings also include our parents. Have you ever asked yourself whether what you absorb is good or bad? I am doubtful. And have you considered how critical this can be for your future career, and life as a whole? Again, I am doubtful.

This is the reason why parents have a primary role in child development. Children are not simply to be "parked" in the kindergarten or at school. They must be formed by their parents first-hand. School and teachers can fill in the gaps, obviously, but the core values should always be imprinted by the respective families. That is, to instil the right mindset, and to be well-behaved and good-mannered. What they usually don't teach is that what is right is not necessarily what is easy. There is usually a blurred line between the two, and this raises a big issue: if the parents ignore this difference, how can they possibly teach it to their little ones? This is the reason they don't. Or rather, children see how their parents normally act and learn how to behave accordingly, and if parents choose the safest route, do the bare minimum, or take short-cuts all the time, guess what will happen? Exactly. The little ones will grow up acting the same.

One of the most difficult things for children to learn and for parents to teach is to never compromise your values, and to stand your ground as far as your beliefs are concerned. It is easy to be like a bird, going where the wind blows, and to changing your views, beliefs and behavior according to the most favorable circumstances. This explains why the world is full of individuals wearing a mask. They claim one thing, but are thinking the opposite. They pretend all the time, rather than being genuine, or they behave in the way others want and expect of them. For example, school bullies are not bad at their core. They choose to play the part because they want to appear cool and strong to others. The sad bit is that it is difficult to maintain dignity and morals when someone changes masks or plays parts according to this or that circumstance.

The real mission is to be consistent, to be uncompromised, despite the situation, person, or event of the moment. This means that if you were taught specific values, you behave according to those, even if they won't necessarily make you the source of much admiration.

The worst decision one can ever make is to question one's values and customize them according to what and who is around them. It is no surprise that we live in a world of suffering, in which a few bad apples can impact entire communities. Parents play a key role in this respect. Since children's minds are like an unseeded garden, it is the parents' duty to plant good seeds, in the form of good manners and true values. With these good values, respect, ethics and dignity should always play a key role. More important, a person's values must not be for sale, meaning that regardless of the circumstances or potential advantages, one shouldn't do something if it contradicts one's principles, nor should one act the way someone else expects if it means sacrificing dignity. Why so? Because values are more important than anyone's acceptance or opinion of you. Therefore, even if I may be excluded from a group of people, at least I will be at peace with my own conscience. I hope you get the point.

Unfortunately, all too often the world goes the other way round. Violence, bullying, and cheating are taking place before our eyes because of a complete lack of values and morality.

In order to gain something convenient to him, my poor-minded father would easily put his dignity, or coherence, or pride on the side. He was the type of person to say yes to superiors, even when they were completely wrong, and would bow his head to others for personal gain. From a tender age, he taught me that it was normal to do so, in order to be competitive in the job market. This is something Mary was always set against, that is, to settle for less, however and wherever. She would not tolerate it if I succumbed to working for free, being underpaid, or making any sort of compromise to my detriment. In short, she did all she could to teach me that dignity is unquestionable, and the same went for respect and pride. Also, she would teach me something from the sacred texts that nowadays have been pretty much cast into oblivion: *"Do unto others as you would have them do unto you"*

(Matthew 7:12; Luke 6:31). It is fair to say that Mary is not a firm believer in religion, but she was brought up learning some of the most famous statements from the Bible in school. Also, she made a point of passing them on to me as part of my upbringing.

This is how I was luckily brought up to be a respectful and well-mannered person. I would slip up, yes, but also I would learn something from it. I learned to admit that no one is perfect, and that it is fine to make mistakes, as long as they are not intentional. I am saying this because those who habitually deceive, lie, or do things under the table, claim to be perfect and flawless all the time. They wish to appear so, at least. They will trade their values for instant favors or personal advantage. Again, while it is the school's duty to provide pupils with an education, it is the parents' imperative to equip their kids with strong basics, which include values, good behavior, and respect, not to mention dignity and strong ethics, which are fundamental to becoming good adults.

If we had more rich-minded parents there would surely be less bullying, cheating, violence, or less bad behavior all around us in general. Because so many poor-minded parents never give their children a real upbringing, in the belief that the school will do the entire job for them, this partly explains why there is such ignorance and widespread bad conduct.

Be a rich-minded person (and parent) yourself:

When it comes to personal gain, ask yourself: does it go in line with my principles? Dignity and ethics should not be questioned, even when it can make you lose credibility and visibility. It is not a matter of pride, but one of sticking to the values you were brought up with. If you are a parent, be a person of good morals like Mary. Learn to say NO when someone deserves a NO. Have the courage to disagree when someone is wrong, or is not in line with your thinking. Too many nod their heads out of fear and cowardice, because they lack the guts to speak up when something is ethically wrong. Put your values first and teach your children to do likewise. As a current or future parent, this is one of the best things you can ever instil in your little ones: *to habitually think critically and speak up*.

SELF-CARE: MIND, BODY, AND SOUL

"Self-care is giving the world the best of you,
Instead of what's left of you."
—Katie Reed, co-founder and CEO of Balanced

Taking care of oneself is essential to leading a better life. Feeling alive and full of vitality is necessary to becoming better versions of ourselves. The more technologically advanced we become, though, the more complacent and lazier we seem to get. Everywhere, people are dragging their feet (especially in the morning), doing their best to make it through to the weekend. This behavior is not only synonymous with energy drainage, but it also indicates a serious lack of vitality, starting from within. Whenever we switch on the TV, we run into all sorts of commercials for vitamins, supplements and special medicines, all claiming to be able to solve our problems, including our lack of energy. Even if these seem to offer a solution, the most they can do is provide temporary relief – temporary because we need to fall back on them continuously. Why is it that we have this recurrent problem with energy?

The answer lies in our life's rhythms, and the bad habits we have instilled within ourselves over the years. If we worry a lot, for instance, we struggle to fall asleep. If we eat unhealthily, we feel drowsy. If we are not properly organized, we waste a lot of time on trivialities. This is how we lack time, focus and, more importantly, *energy*.

You will agree that having a constant lack of energy is not normal. Waking up in the morning and already feeling exhausted is even less normal. We may feel drowsy after lunch and turn to coffee. We may be carrying a few extra pounds and use low calorie foods or drinks in an effort to control our weight. Similarly, if we feel exhausted, we may fall back on supplements as a result. Again, these are not real problem-solvers. You may receive a temporary relief, that's true, but no temporary solution is a real solution. Why is that? If you think of your car, for instance, and have it repaired by a mechanic, do you expect it to function for a long time or just a couple of days? Why, then, are we happy with only temporary relief when it comes to our bodies? This explains the extensive usage of medicines, energy drinks, and coffee. Instead, to have constant energy, we should take care of ourselves more often and more seriously. Basically, we must look after ourselves by dedicating adequate time to restoring our body, mind and soul.

Below are the three elements; I thought it might be useful to go through all of them respectively.

THE BODY

The body refers to our physical condition – our bodily health and its overall wellness with no illnesses or pain of sorts. In order to function optimally, you need to do some proper physical activities and literally get moving. The lack of energy is due, in the case of the body, to a lack of physical movement, and a careless diet made up of what's tasty instead of what's healthy. In fact, rarely is what is delicious also healthy for the organism. The heavier your meal, the more energy your organs will need to digest it. The way it does this is by robbing the other parts of the body of said energy to digest what is in your stomach. This is why we feel tired and sleepy after generous portions of calorific, delicious food. Ideally, you should change your culinary habits by filling yourself up with more vegetables and fewer animal proteins. This will prevent the organism from stealing precious energy from the rest of the body. Regular physical activity is as important to keep fit, slim and, more importantly, *alive*. Do not neglect your body, as you are blessed with one, and one only. Do not take it for granted.

THE MIND

Being in good physical shape is important, but a fit body requires a sound mind to function properly. We simply can't go that far when our body is healthy but our mind is not, or vice versa. Similarly, our shiny new car won't take us far if we don't take proper care of its inner mechanisms. The same goes for the organism. How does one nurture the mind? The answer lies in controlling what you let into it, and this can be achieved by being very selective as to what you focus your attention on and decide to read. Books made up of fascinating ideas and nuggets of wisdom are a case in point. You will agree that while some books are just meant to be read, others are to be devoured completely, and the latter is what I am referring to. Being very selective with what you let in, in terms of knowledge and information, will certainly influence your current thinking and future actions for the better or the worse. A great mind is not God's gift reserved for only a few, nor is one born as a genius. I am strongly convinced that everyone has the potential to build a powerful mind and great ideas, if only they would nurture it more often with selective content. Trashy magazines won't do the trick, nor will the newspapers. Full of negativity and biased opinions, these surely won't lift you up. After all, how can the daily news of economic instability, earthquakes, or the world famine give you the positivity you so need to push yourself beyond the limits? Informing ourselves about what's going on is important, of course, but filling your head with a daily dose of negative news won't do you any good. If anything, it can turn you into a more pessimistic, depressed person, and a negative mind won't benefit you at all. So, switch off your TV, and turn your attention to some well-written books – food for thought, as they say. This type of content will provide you with a boost of positivity and creativity.

After being selective with books, do the same with the people you let into your life. As human beings, we are so easily influenced by whatever and whoever is around us. They say that we tend to become the average of the five people we spend most time with. Personally speaking, I have to admit that this is true. As individuals can heavily shape us, do yourself a favor and choose to whom you will most wisely dedicate your time. Are you sceptical about this? If pessimists surround you, aren't you likely to become one in time? For sure you will. If your friends are big spenders, will money not burn a hole in your pocket, too? Of course it will. And lastly, if you are always in the company of poor-minded people like Tony, who think that the world is all about surviving and not thriving, will you not be pushed to think that way, too? You can answer that yourself. Negative thinking is like a virus, and it is a tough one to eradicate. My poor-minded dad was always thinking negatively, like when he would save up without ever enjoying a little bit of it. Not surprisingly, Tony and Mary were usually arguing about finances. Tony would save and save for rainy days, while Mary would be sensible with her money and use it for quality times with her family.

So, as with books, choose your people carefully; their thinking can lift you up as well as get you down. While friends can easily come in and out of your life, what should you do when the attitude of a spouse, or a family member is bringing you down? It is miles harder to ignore someone living under the same roof – more difficult, but not impossible. If you think that one or both of your parents are bringing you down with their average or pessimistic thinking, for your own sake, reduce your time spent with them as much as possible. It may feel unnatural to do so because they are still your family. If you hold your self-growth dear, it is for your own sake that you should minimize your company with complainers, downers, and naysayers. This is what I did myself. When I realized that the influence of my poor-minded dad was steering me towards a life of mediocrity, I took up steering clear of him, and ignoring his counsel at every occasion. Deep down, I knew that the less time I was spending with a conventional person, and the more time I spent in the company of my rich-minded mom, the more I would benefit, in terms of positivity, creativity, and productivity. If you also find yourself surrounded with negative or average people, for the welfare of your mind, stay away from them as often as possible. However hard it may seem at first, this decision will pay off in the long run. Soon, you will figure out that all those "can't do" attitudes were just a projection of your friends' and parents' minds, not yours. As Dwayne Johnson would put it, "If someone tells you, 'you can't', they are showing you their limits, not yours."[12] Simply put, what they think they cannot do is only valid to them. What is a limit to them is not necessarily limiting for you, too. Keep this in mind next time someone tries to drag you down.

THE SOUL

Other than the body to take care of, and the mind to be constantly fed, the soul is perhaps the most ignored of all. As we know, we are made up of a body and a mind, but also a soul. Even though we cannot see the latter, no one can deny that we have one. Yet, it is so often ignored, mainly giving room for personal gain and instant gratification. Now, a lack of values equates to a poor soul. Incoherence with one's beliefs and values is indicative of inner instability. Deep down, we can distinguish what is good from what is bad. We also know what is morally acceptable and what is not. Yet, we make all manner of compromises to justify our actions, both good and bad. What about ethics in these cases? They are simply put to the side. When we lack values, have a weak will, and are in the habit of always justifying ourselves morally and ethically, this is a sign of a fragile soul. Have you perhaps read *The Portrait of Dorian Gray* by Oscar Wilde? It is the story of a handsome, wealthy and pure-hearted guy who eventually became cruel and corrupted in the pursuit of personal satisfaction and advantage. This should act as a strong reminder as to why it is so important not to compromise our morality for personal gain.

How can we keep our soul alive and strong within our own body? One of the best ways is to become a giving person who is generous and available. Mary was a natural giver. Her nature was that of a giving, caring person, without necessarily expecting something back. The simple act of serving and being the first to help out is so fulfilling to the soul; it makes one feel so good that it is almost impossible to describe. Have you ever experienced that feeling of ecstasy when you simply make someone's day? That's because the more you help, the more you enrich your soul. Also, meditation can help in this respect. Meditating is, in fact, a great source for finding inner peace and feeding one's soul. If you are undecided as to what type of meditation to pick up first, try a few different types and then pick the one that suits you the most.

No living creature can be helpful to others if they are not initially sound themselves. The Bible itself speaks about vitality, but to be vital, you need energy, and to have energy, you need to take care of yourself, starting with your body, your mind, and especially your soul. Only then can you be an example to those around you.

Be a rich-minded person (and parent) yourself:

Take care of your body, mind, and soul. You have so much to gain from doing so. This is a necessary step towards personal greatness, starting from the inside. Some useful tips were described above. Read and re-read the three sections regarding the body, the mind, and the soul. Make sure the messages between the lines get in...and *stay in*. Apply them and you will become one hundred percent better, both outwardly and inwardly. Only when you are at peace with yourself can you then be a model to others. Someone who hasn't taken the time to work on himself or herself first cannot hope to become an example to others, both as a person or a parent. So, work on your mind, body, and soul to be the rich-minded person you so deserve to be. Don't play the average role. Don't be part of the club.

SELF-REWARDING TO KEEP YOU MOTIVATED

"It's the small wins on the long journey
that we need in order to keep our
confidence, joy, and motivation alive."
—Brendon Burchard, author, motivational speaker

One of the hardest things I've experienced was keeping myself motivated long enough to do all the things I had on my plate – to get the s**t done without letting distractions get in the way. Be mindful here. By this I do not necessarily mean work; I consider my personal stuff as important as the job. I say this because while working may be important to pay bills and earn a living, becoming a better version of yourself is as crucial (at least to me), if not even more so. What makes life fulfilling is not a salary raise or ascending the career ladder, rather it is *progressing on a personal level.* If you disagree with this, let me ask you a legitimate question: will having a higher position make you feel better? At first, perhaps it might. You may be earning more and you may increase your status, but let's be honest, you will also have more stress, pressure, and responsibilities on your shoulders. The outcome? Less time for your family, and very little energy left for your days off. Furthermore, earning more has proved to be at odds with lasting happiness. Usually, those with a very good salary tend to treat themselves more often with better commodities, trendy clothes, a nicer house, a powerful car, you name it. The issue is that by habitually treating themselves, they also increase their overall expenses, ending up with next to nothing at the end of the month. You can see for yourself how delusional it is to crave more money. At the end of the day, it won't give you more free time or financial independence.

To me, *happiness is all about doing what you love.* I strive to improve on a personal level, both inside and outside the workplace, and the feeling of progression is priceless from a personal point of view. Have you ever experienced that feeling of being tired, yet very satisfied in the evening? Have you felt you have reached a sense of completeness deep inside? That's what I call *happiness*, which goes hand-in-hand with *fulfilment.* The Japanese use the word *ikigai*. That is, being happy while being busy. This is to be occupied, but with a clear purpose in mind, a direction toward which to lead your effort, time and, more important, your life. By contrast, in the Western world being busy has always had a negative connotation. "I am busy, so I can't do what I would like to do," or, "I am tied up all week, so I have no time." That said, there are two kinds of busyness: one that makes you fulfil your duty, which is usually uninspiring and forced by outer circumstances, and another that makes you feel complete, satisfied and most of all, fulfilled, regardless of the time you put in. In my view, there is nothing more appealing and satisfactory than being happy with what you do daily, to have your *ikigai* clear in your mind working *for* you rather than against you. Now, people complain about having no time at all, while the truth is rather a misuse of it. In fact, by simply clearing up your mind and reorganizing your daily schedule, you will be more than capable of scraping some hours off every day and every week for what you really like, be it a hobby, a passion, your family, or even a future business idea. Other than time, we also have to deal with our lack of persistence when things get tough. This is how we are and how we stay unfulfilled again and again, and mistakenly postpone what we could do today until our retirement.

Motivation is essential, not just for us to get started, but also to keep us going when things get challenging. For instance, I think that everyone out there has the skills to write their own book, start their own business, commence their dream project, and so on. The great majority give up easily and quickly, because while most of us have a peak in motivation at first, like a phone battery, it decreases as time progresses. Also, without a *plan of action*, which is crucial, one won't get anything done. This is how we almost always give up along the way, not only ending up with nothing complete, but also with a deep inner sense of disappointment. For instance, why is it that a majority of people fail to follow a diet plan? The simple reason is that they don't really put in the effort and the constancy required to get proper results. They are determined in the beginning, but the motivation trails off after a couple of weeks. Again, like the waning phone battery, motivation drains with the passing of time. This holds true not just for fitness, but for any worthy objectives passing through our minds.

While people blame this on time, family, or their frenetic schedules, they should rather point the finger at themselves and their lack of discipline. Motivation can be compared to the gas you put into your car. At the start of the ride, the car's tank is full to the brim. As the day progresses, the tank gradually empties out. You will be aware that old cars consume more gas, getting empty quicker. The same applies to a person's motivation. While it is high at the start of a project or a task, it gradually gets lower over time. It gets even lower and drops faster if they miss a proper plan of execution. This is why you constantly need to feed your motivation, especially when things get tough, because, it is mainly during the lows that our motivation is severely put to the test, and could be at risk of disappearing completely.

This explains why we procrastinate, fall behind, and end up doing much less than we could. As a solution, I repeat this mantra every day:

Today is going to be a great day.

Today is going to be a productive day.

Today is going to rock.

I repeat this mantra at least three times a day. To me, this is the magic number to convince myself that today will actually be a day worth living. Almost everyone dreads Mondays, dreaming of the weekend instead. When someone complains all the time, they are simply thinking aloud, expressing what's in their heads. Since what we say can not only substantially influence our mood, but also our subconscious, I'd rather talk positively, lifting up my subconscious rather than bringing it down. In practical terms, rather than saying, "Oh, my gosh, it is Monday tomorrow," I would rather say, "No matter if it is Monday, I will make it great anyway." The more I repeat this, the more convinced I become. The more I believe this to be true, the more likely it will become *my reality*. The whole point of speaking positively is to turn something I want into something concrete. As the few lines above indicate, I want to have a great day not just in words, but also in reality.

If you ask around, most people will tell you they wish to be happy, or they would do anything to be happy. Well, while in words it can be so, in everyday life, the story is slightly different:

We all want to be unconditionally happy, but we carry a backpack full of conditions.

Continuing to reason in this way will only make you miserable. Because perfect conditions do not exist, at least in this world, we complain around the clock about what's going wrong. Be it the weather, the neighbors, or the traffic, this is how we get off to a bad start that lasts from the minute we wake up until the moment we go to bed. How can we be motivated if the negative conditions, standards, and parameters we set constantly influence us? This is the reason I decided to start off my day by repeating the above mantra. In my view:

No matter the people or the circumstances,
it is going to be a great day. Period.

If you repeat the above sentence a few times, positivity will start flowing into your veins almost instantly. Rather than reasoning like the great majority of ordinary people who start off pessimistically and wait for happy conditions to knock on their doors, I decided to cheer up from the word go, and let my initial optimism influence circumstances all around me. I began to use positive vibes, rather than negative ones to impact the outer world, because motivation thrives with a positive mindset. Subsequently, with motivation on your side, commitment and constancy will follow. If you take part in a marathon, for example, you have a positive feeling that you will get to the finish line. You would never start a race, or any other competition for that matter, prophesying that you will not succeed. Having a powerful mantra in your arsenal is key to giving yourself the powerful, positive attitude that everyone needs, but very few obtain.

My father was one of the many who would start off the day with pessimism, until favorable conditions were met. As usual, they never were, since he made a point of starting off on the wrong foot. He was always discontent for one reason or another because he let the outside control his thoughts and feelings, rather than managing outer events with a strong, positive attitude. By contrast, Mary believed that despite the fact that life can be hard and unfair sometimes, we should always find a reason to be happy and grateful. Many years later, I can say that she was completely right. I learned to condition my perspective on the outside world with a positive attitude coming from the inside, and that really worked magic.

Motivation can be hard to get hold of first thing in the morning. Even so, once we finally have it, we must keep ourselves motivated all through the day. At any time, we can give up on what we are doing, leaving unfinished tasks and projects on the plate. As we all know, things left undone can turn out to be completely useless. Many famous painters in history, such as Leonardo da Vinci, left us unfinished masterpieces. They had so much going on in their heads that they were grappling considerably with motivation to keep themselves going. So, as you see, no one is really immune from motivational struggle. Even geniuses of the likes of da Vinci had a problem with maintaining enough motivation to finish what was on his easel before moving on to something new. This is why I repeatedly say that starting off with something is super easy. Keeping it going is another story.

The common rule out there is that we are rewarded at the end of projects, or the calendar year. Having tried this myself many times, I have found it does not really work. With the reward being so far away, people can't help getting easily burned out. What's the point of celebrating when you are too tired, have a headache, or simply lack any energy? Exactly. You don't feel like it. Commemorating your achievements when you are fresh is much more enjoyable, versus when you are mentally or physically exhausted. Personally, when I am worn out, all I want to do is be on my own and binge watch TV, feeling like doing nothing else.

Celebrating at the end of something is not always the best option, but if you still want to reward yourself for having the job done, you can do so by celebrating in-between your everyday duties. In doing so, you compliment yourself on what you have accomplished so far, by treating yourself to a nice dinner, a trip outdoors, some shopping, or whatever you fancy. It can be any sort of mini reward for something important that you have bagged; just remember to do so in moderation. This is why I call them mini rewards, and while they may be mini, the lift they can give you is extraordinary. It is a genuine congratulations card for your finished duty, and a boost for what is coming next. If you disagree with getting recurrent rewards, rather than just one in the end, consider dogs as an example. Have you ever wondered how police train dogs to detect drugs? It all starts when they are puppies. They are taught to find drugs as a game. They are taught to find the white tissue (that piece of rolled cloth you may have seen on TV), and whenever they find it, the trainer praises them. How? With some nice words, a pat, and of course, some food. The dogs keep doing a good job because they know their trainer will reward them whenever they find some drugs. This motivates the dogs to get going and, more importantly, keep going. The dogs do not realize how important their job is, nor do they consider it a duty or an obligation to find drug smugglers at the airport. To them, it is just a game, so they set out with the knowledge that they will receive a treat anytime they find the "hidden stuff." They are not instructed to scout out ten individuals for drugs before being rewarded, nor do they have to meet performance metrics before receiving their prize. Anytime they find a drug, they promptly get a small win because the trainer knows that this treatment keeps the dogs exited and motivated to keep the job (or game) going.

By contrast, in companies, we are obsessed with numbers and metrics, yet the only reward we get is the wage. Having worked for numerous companies, I can guarantee that the mere wage attached to end-of-year numbers is not very motivating, nor does it mean that employees always try their hardest.

If the above motivational training works for animals, why not model them? Why not reward yourself along the way, rather than just once? Treat yourself on a continuous basis, so you'll stay inspired to keep going. If we think about it, we are very ignorant in the field of motivation. Rarely do we get a smile, or pat on the shoulder from our superiors. Instead, all we get is the reminder that "we are just doing our jobs." I bet everyone has been told this at least once. Rather than complaining when things go wrong, and saying nothing when they go well, we should learn to compliment people like dog trainers do with their pets. As motivation is not on tap, and we don't often get it at work from our superiors, try this: 1) repeat a personal mantra to yourself, and 2) reward yourself with small wins. In doing so, you will keep your motivation up and running. Now you know how to unlock yourself and pursue what's been on hold for all too long.

Be a rich-minded person (and parent) yourself:

Getting started is dead easy when it comes to personal goals and projects. Being consistent is a different ball game. We fail to persist because we either don't have a plan, or our initial motivation drops over time. This is why nursing your motivational side is essential to keeping yourself going, regardless of what happens along the way. Speaking to yourself a certain way

– such as repeating a personal mantra – can certainly work. In addition, treating yourself from time to time before the end of your project is also an important factor in sustaining momentum to finish up what you have started. This can greatly benefit you and keep you from getting stuck, especially when your patience and determination are really put to the test. In the same way that we nurture our bodies, so should we nurture our inner motivation. Make use of frequent rewards until you reach completion of your task. You are now reading this finished book because I personally put these techniques into practice. Nothing more, nothing less. It was no mean feat, I admit, yet if I managed to do it, so can you.

FAMILY FIRST

"I don't care how hard being together is,
nothing is worse than being apart."
—Josephine Angelini, author of young adult fiction

In a society where people continually wear a mask, family becomes increasingly vital to fulfil our need for affection. In fact, the more we bump into fake individuals, the more we should deem family important. Why? Because with so many opportunists around us, parents become our safety net; they provide us with someone to trust and turn to. Not only do they not wear masks – or so they shouldn't – but also they are always present in the moment of need – or so they should be. This is why genuine parental affection is so important in this chaotic world and should never be taken for granted.

Sadly, Tony would never give Mary and me the pride of place. Being a workaholic all along, his job at the restaurant was his only concern in life. Working can be important to earn a living, to invest in education, and save up for rainy days, but other than that, *we should work to live, not live to work.* As a poor-minded parent, he mistakenly thought, like many parents out there, that life can only be enjoyed after retirement. The so-called "golden years," as the term suggests, indeed permit one to have more time and money at one's disposal, but listening to what the elderly have to say, these years do not seem very golden after all. In fact, they often complain about body pain, constant tiredness, and long recovery times, to name a few. It is true that work may be a distant memory to them, but after a while, many would readily switch places and get back to work. Why? Simply out of boredom and to have a daily routine again.

If you ask me, this is a bit of a paradox. When people are young, they claim they don't have the time and the money to do all the things they would like to do. Then, when the same people are happily retired, they complain about all sorts of ailments and don't have the energy for all of their grand plans.

This is a mistake Mary wanted to avoid like the plague. To her, family came first. Period! Not money or work, but family moments were what mattered. Of course, we need some money to live comfortably, but precious family memories are what we should truly treasure, as they only occur once. This was also one of the reasons Mary and Tony eventually divorced. While one would focus solely on work, work, and more work, the other would both work and look for moments to spend with family. My parents also relied on babysitters to fill voids, but that was not the solution. No one can really replace family and the moments that are being created within one. Dear reader, if you, like Tony, also think that money and a career play a primary role in family life, bear in mind that this comes at a cost. As stated earlier, there is always a price to pay for every choice we make, and sometimes that price can be extremely high. When we hear, "Life is too short," or, "Time flies," this simply reminds us that we have limited time to do what really matters — travelling, discovering, enjoying ourselves, and so on. Why place work and money over family, children, and even one's dreams?

To any workaholics out there who are obsessed with careers and money, be mindful that this comes at the detriment of the rest of your family. For instance, children will spend little time with you and more moments at their grandparents' place or with the babysitter. Result? They eventually grow up and you end up not knowing your kids anymore. Sad, but true. Parents usually justify themselves by pointing the finger at a shortage of money and time. They claim to not have been born rich, and the like. Regardless of what they say, let's not forget that parents are children's prime educators. If they are absent for the most part, how much time do they carve out for their little ones? Technology and video calls can compensate, at least partially, but you will agree that nothing replaces an in-person interaction, or a face-to-face conversation. So again, working and pursuing a career are important, as is a monthly paycheck. Just don't be a workaholic like Tony. That is, don't sacrifice family time for the job and money. As time is limited, and we are granted only one life and one childhood, don't make the mistake of postponing family time indefinitely. Like birds, children eventually grow up and "leave the nest" for good. When that moment arrives, you will be left mainly with memories in your head, photos on your walls and phones to fill the void. All of those moments spent together camping, fishing, and hiking will be proof of how present — or absent — you were as a parent, not the sum of bucks you have accumulated over the years. Far better are all the quality moments you have spent together. Money is necessary, you may argue, as it finances everything, education included. True, but nowadays it is much easier to get scholarships and enroll in college or university. On the contrary, time does not rewind. Once it is gone, it is gone for good; there is no rewind button to click. This is when regrets get the better of us. When we start feeling guilty for all the things we could have done with our sons or daughters but didn't. It is when we were too occupied with working overtime to meet the company's metrics and targets that we have deep regrets. We know crying over spilt milk is of no use, but we postpone indefinitely what we could be doing today. That said, be more proactive. Careers are important for numerous reasons, but, personally, nothing compares a Christmas event or an end-of-year party with one's family members.

Remember that the years to enjoy with your offspring are quite limited. Do not let their childhood bypass you like a gust of wind because you were too occupied and never at home.

It is never too late for those
that want to change for the better,
provided that they act TODAY.

Be a rich-minded person (and parent) yourself:

To the rich-minded, family love comes first. They know there is nothing more enriching than nurtured relationships and being caring, especially to loved ones. This is what makes a parent rich deep down, not the money they may have accumulated over the years, or the certificates on the wall, but the family photos that surround them and the joyous memories they hold dear. The person who cares about their loved ones, and finds time for them, will never be completely alone, notably when things take a bad turn. By contrast, materialistic individuals, who mainly take care of themselves and their personal goals, are unaware of how empty their lives really are. Take away their job title and status, and their lives become meaningless and purposeless. Not surprisingly, the latter are more apt to suffer from loneliness, especially during bank holidays and other special occasions. Why? Because they never put in the necessary effort to create meaningful relationships with family and close friends. We all have the same twenty-four hours a day, the same seven days a week. If you have been a very busy parent up until now, re-manage your time and scrape some hours off every week to stay close with your loved ones. Believe me, this will enrich your life like nothing else.

FAMILY FIRST (SECOND PART)

"One day you will wake up and there won't be any more time to do the things you've always wanted. Do it now."
—Paulo Coelho, Brazilian lyricist and novelist

Having a family, and giving it priority, are the first steps to living a quality life. At the end of your life, it will be the sum of all your quality memories that really count. It is the uniqueness of precious moments that will make you say, "This was a life worth living." Especially when old age takes its toll, one tends to look back and sum up how well or how badly they have lived up to that point. You may have heard of a mid-life crisis, when someone who is in their forties or fifties suddenly feels lost, and wonders, "What the heck am I doing with my life?" This is typical of those who never really enjoyed life as they should have or expected to. As said earlier, too focused on meeting numbers, goals and promotions, many ambitious individuals always put their duty first, to the detriment of all the rest, including loved ones, friendships, and life as a whole. These people usually reason in the following way:

1. When I earn more money, I will…
2. When I pay off my mortgage, I will…
3. When my children grow up and move out, I will…

If you haven't noticed, this kind of reasoning is all about postponing to some indefinite time in the future what we are meant to do *today*, but without ever specifying *when*. We keep telling ourselves that we will be better off when a condition is met, be it monetary, children not yet being independent, and so on. Most of us tend to make a pact with ourselves to make this happen or to make that change only after something else occurs. Because of this so-called deal we make, we unconsciously make time pass as quickly as possible. This happens because, believe it or not, we are the CEOs of our lives. If time flies so quickly, it is because we wanted it to. Don't you believe so? When we want Christmas or the holidays to arrive quickly, we are unconsciously asking the sun and moon to fast-track time, and usually it happens.

Rather than stating that time flies, we should start asking ourselves these questions: Am I enjoying my life? Am I living or just surviving throughout my best years? Am I doing all the things I am meant to do before it is too late?

It is better to ask critical questions, rather than simply making statements such as, "I am always broke;" "I am terrible," and the like. If we do, we will feel condemned by default. We will be under the impression that things are static, irremovable, and must be accepted for what they are, as if it was God's will. Worse, we chain ourselves to this or that situation, usually hard and unpleasant, through continual and internal repetitions. This is how we convince ourselves, for instance, that we are bad at this and rubbish at that, or that we are disorganized, untidy, and thus hopeless. Unfortunately, this is how we create our own glass ceilings – our invisible prisons – forever and ever, without realizing they are self-made.

Tony was exactly like this. Working all year round with no days off, he used to spend only a few weeks at Christmas at his own parents' (my grandparents) place. Certainly, those were well-deserved holidays, but that was all. He was of the opinion that one can enjoy one's savings and life as a whole, only after retiring, not realizing that when sons and daughters turn into adults, they eventually move out. That also means moments with the original family become rarer and rarer. This is why Mary was taking every given opportunity to spend quality moments with the family. She used to do so by taking some time off to go on trips, not only to enjoy good times, but also to pile up nice memories for when she would be alone again. She didn't reason like Tony, postponing every summer, Christmas, or Easter with excuses like, "We will go, but later on," or, "There is no money now; we cannot afford it." Yes, it is true that money can get low, but even so, Mary was so determined to find it one way or another that she used to ask her boss to work overtime whenever possible. In this sense, she was a very determined person who left no space for excuses in achieving what she wanted. And you too, dear person reading this, remember that:

> *Determination is key to everything.*
> *Excuses are not. They may make*
> *you feel forgiven, but never fulfilled.*

Tony was stingy by nature, so Mary's choice of working overtime was not really an option, because in his opinion, even that money she earned shouldn't go towards what she wanted so badly: extra money to make me happy. You may be wondering at this point, what do Tony and Mary actually have in common? That's a question I also asked myself on numerous occasions, and every time I could not find an answer, due in part to my young age. No wonder they got divorced in the end, and no surprise that most of my memories of trips and summer times were with my mother and relatives only. Being an adult myself now, I can sum it up this way:

- ➤ My rich-minded mom wanted to carve out some time to have quality moments with her son, and so she did.
- ➤ My poor-minded dad didn't really want to subtract time and profit from work, and that's what he did, too.

The daily choices we make are a serious matter. Unconsciously or not, we compromise and make agreements all the time. We act on them, and the results eventually show up. If someone is a workaholic, that's a choice; if someone is bad, or selfish, or unprincipled, that's a decision; and if someone is a taker and never a giver, that's also a choice – a poor one, but it remains a choice.

It is not really a matter of luck or bad luck; it is rather a question of what we decide to prioritize. My rich-minded mother considered family time a priority. My poor-minded father deemed work a priority, and not just out of necessity. To him, it was normal to intentionally put anything else second. In his view, one had to accumulate as much money as possible, and wait to be old enough to enjoy the fruits of one's labor; anything that was not money-related could either be put off or simply dismissed. In my view:

> *Everyone is the master of their own destiny.*
> *What you decide to be a priority, will be.*
> *What you choose not to be a priority, will also be!*

If you ask me, it is not really the lack of time that is the problem, nor is it the lack of money that prevents us from doing what we would like to do. Instead, it is the lack of commitment, the absence of dedication underneath. As Henry Ford is alleged to have put it, "Whether you think you can, or think you can't – you're right." So, it is all a matter of what you think you can or cannot do that matters, because in both cases, you will be right.

In addition, so many mix up busyness with productivity, which is not necessarily the same thing. Busyness is about dealing with low-value stuff, bringing about good results in the now. Productivity involves coping with high-value tasks, bringing about satisfaction and lasting fulfilment. The good thing about the latter is that it can turn your life upside down for the better, if you identify and, more important, act upon it.

The Pareto Principle asserts that 80% is trivial and only 20% is crucial, and being busy versus being productive follows the same logic. Only a tiny percentage of what we do leaves an impact on ourselves and others. The rest is just about keeping us occupied in some way or other. Re-managing our time is key to being less busy, but more productive. Only through this can we carve out more spare time for quality moments with our loved ones. When someone is an avid social media user or watches a number of sitcoms just to keep occupied, that is usually the same person who claims to be too busy for anything else. Now, isn't that a contradiction? You bet it is. When we say we are busy all day long, every day, we should ask ourselves, "What am I busy at?" "Is this or that activity really worth my time?"

Personally speaking, people who endlessly surf the Net or watch movies just to expend time, are in for a poorly lived life. Instead, those who go for a rich life would not waste time on the couch, eating pizzas or snacks every weekend. They would still put their feet up after work, but without doing so out of habit, because when a particular behavior becomes a habit, it is not just repeated on cold winter nights, but at any possible time. This is a shame if we consider that we only have a few years of active, energetic life, and that time is even more limited when it comes to family (in case you are a parent now). Ask yourself more often, "Is what I am doing really worth my time?" "Could I not spend the same hours in a better way, doing something differently?"

Everyone is entitled to lead a rich life. Unless you are part of that tiny percentage who are always on the go, make a habit of asking yourself, "How I am spending my free time? Cleverly or poorly?"

In the absence of such questions, many never live life to the fullest. This also explains why they don't have many memories with friends, acquaintances, and more important, families. Be the rich-minded person you so deserve to be. It is never too late to make up for lost times.

Be a rich-minded person (and parent) yourself:

What type of life are you leading – an enriching existence or a poor one? Just for the record, a rich life is one made up of quality moments with those most dear to us. Living in a digital era notwithstanding, there are no social media that can replace a good old in-person conversation. Personally, I have always travelled for miles to meet up with new and old buddies. Was it worth it? Absolutely. We all know how important networking is, but let's not narrow it down to business only. Despite the word "networking" sounds only virtual and only done online, this is not true. It can be performed both virtually and in the real world, and you can choose which one to go with. Personally, I believe that enriching moments are better when done in-person. It might sound behind the times, but again, no social network, however updated, can beat a nice face-to-face conversation. Make a habit of dropping social media and movies on sunny days and carve out some afternoons or evenings away from your domestic walls. You won't regret it. That's guaranteed.

YOU ARE NOT YOUR GRADES

*"Your grades mean nothing
to your future success."*
**—Rob Dial, founder and host of
The Mindset Mentor**

I don't know about where you live, but in my country (that is, Italy), there is an obsession with grades. To many people, marks come first. If this sounds familiar to you too, don't get me wrong. Getting a good mark is always a nice experience, and something to be proud of. The problem lies in working specifically for the grade, leaving all the rest as a footnote. When we study just for grades, everything becomes legitimate in order to pass with flying colors. At least to students, this is when cheating becomes acceptable because all that matters is attaining a good grade.

Parents and teachers continually remind students that if they don't study, they will damage their future careers. This can be true, but it is likewise bad to grow up in a reality in which grades – not the lessons – are the only thing that count:

**When an objective becomes too central,
the rest tends to be put aside –
and sometimes, even morals and ethics.**

Why is it, for instance, that there are tons of yellow cards issued by the referees during important football matches? And how many footballers make up fake excuses to gain a penalty? Because when the focus is exclusively on the victory (or the grades in education), all seems legitimate to reach one's purpose. "The means justify the end," they say. But what about ethics, fair play, and transparency?

When we used to watch cartoons back in the day, there was always a recurrent theme: *honesty*. We always noticed the protagonist's loyalty, usually from start to finish. By contrast, the enemy used to cheat and play all manner of dirty tricks to win easily. You can see the point here: we tend to sympathize with the protagonist (the kind-hearted guy, who plays fairly from beginning to end), yet we grow up learning to focus on victory and to have good grades, no matter what we choose to do to get there.

Our parents are happy and reward us if we get a good mark on a test, essay, or exam. Likewise, we get reprimanded if we perform badly. So, we are judged, rewarded, or punished not for what we have learned during the term, but rather on how we have scored on essays, tests, and exams. In society as it is now, many employers judge a person by their grades. In the UK, for instance, most jobs require a 1:1 or at least a 2:1 (e.g., "pass with distinction" and "pass with merit," respectively) as a pre-requisite. Other than going through previous work experiences, they give a lot of weight to your marks, as if grades may classify how intelligent or stupid you are. Thus, unless you get one of the above grades, you are easily screened out. So, in some ways we cannot really blame parents here for giving too much weight to marks.

In fact, putting too much emphasis on grades does not define a person for their talents, aptitudes, or lack thereof. Just because one may be bad at math or other scientific subjects does not make him or her stupid. He or she may still be talented at the arts or other non-scientific fields such as literature or philosophy. Besides, who are we to state that some subjects are more important than others? It is true that some areas are more requested in the job world, giving more opportunities to find good employment, but other than that, this does not make any subject second to none. Who said that gymnastics is less important than English literature? And who established that religion is trivial compared to economics? Some will give more opportunities, but in terms of lessons learned, again, no subject is better than any other.

Aside from employers, this also seems unclear to many parents. They demand their boys and girls be good at all subjects, often stressing some areas over others. Additionally, they put a great deal of pressure on them in order to get good — even excellent — marks to secure themselves a place in this college or that university. Unconsciously or not, this is how grades become central to how we judge a person. As said above, getting a good mark is always a pleasant experience — something to be cheerful about. The issue arises when it becomes the focal point for employers, HRs, and parents alike. I have never heard a person or parent ask their kids what lessons they picked up from this or that class, only how well or how badly they performed, always in terms of marks, of course.

If we take into consideration some Harvard dropouts (the likes of Mark Zuckerberg, Bill Gates and many others), they made bigger fortunes as university dropouts than as graduates with excellent grades. And there is more to it; they are now in positions of command and earn more than all of their former classmates combined. Similarly, I know of many non-graduate peers who became self-employed, exploited that aptitude, and are now well-off. Other than the economic factor, they have something I deem priceless: *personal satisfaction*. They love what they do, in a nutshell. By contrast, their graduate peers earn less, and are more likely to work in a job they hate.

Similarly, Thomas Edison and Albert Einstein were no less inclined to studying. While they were initially judged and criticized, it was their original ideas, not their grades, that made a substantial difference. They were evaluated and rewarded by their ability to take risks. Also, rather than memorizing facts, dates and ideas in class, they used their own creative powers instead of following the old formula: *study hard, get decent grades, so you can find a good job.*

It is not grades that dictate who you are.
It is your creativity to think outside the box.

Intensive study is very often something about which parents remind their sons and daughters. Obey the teacher. Do well in class. Get your diploma. Find a good occupation and settle down. This is what an average parent would tell their children. They unconsciously behave so, for the simple fact that they were taught likewise in their childhood. Now that they are parents themselves, they put forward the same model, in the belief that this is how things are supposed to be. To many, it is safer to stick to the established rules, rather than create their own. It is much safer to avoid creativity, which is full of uncertainties, and rely instead on what already exists and usually has been set by others. Why? Because choosing from available options does not imply risks, and if there are some, they are very limited. This is why conforming to rules is the preferred route by teachers and parents alike. The other option, that is, creating your own opportunities, implies all manner of risks and a high rate of failure. Because of this, it is usually the least chosen road.

Why is it that so many people panic easily, while others manage to stay calm and hold their nerve when things take a bad turn? Because, while the former are not used to risks and unexpected surprises, the latter are so used to being pushed to the limits that they are not bothered by it anymore. Hands-on experience, not grades, gave these people the ability to keep standing in the face of difficulties, becoming stronger versions of themselves. If you are ambitious, you should aim at becoming one of these people, too.

Be a rich-minded person (and parent) yourself:

While marks can easily classify a person's current knowledge, they do not provide a thorough image of someone. Yet, in many cases, this is how people are usually judged. Also, grades imply memorizing concepts in order to do well on exams, but this does not always ensure that those very concepts are actually understood by the student. Never mind their being put into practice in everyday vicissitudes. Reality is our true teacher – the one to test us on a constant basis. It won't give us grades or pats on the shoulder, but all kinds of feedback and endless kicks in the butt instead. In short, making mistakes is the best teacher, and where lessons are really learned. Pain is never pleasant and neither is failure. This is why being a fast learner, and keeping your eyes open, are "musts" if you want to avoid the same mistakes again and again. That said, pay less attention to your grades. Focus more on what you have learned from past events. As marks don't really define who you are, nor where you want to go, make a point of treasuring the lessons that events always bring along with them. Those are the real thing.

LEARN TO SAY 'NO'

*"It's only by saying 'NO' that you can concentrate
on the things that are really important."*
**—Steve Jobs, co-founder,
chairman, CEO of Apple®**

One of the hardest things we can ever do is learn to say NO. Not climbing a mountain or running marathons. Not even following a strict diet or writing a dissertation. Simply saying a plain, but firm NO!

I can already hear many of you disagree with this. This is understandable. However, I have experienced that nothing is as challenging as learning to say NO in a polite, but decisive way. In short, to have an iron will. This is because while we tend to disagree, we do it in a way that is far too weak. For instance, when someone is pushy, an initial NO can oftentimes become a YES. If you look at marketing data, a great deal of sales are made thanks to the so-called "nagging factor." Think of children who habitually nag their parents to get what they want. They go to the supermarket or mall, for example, see an eye-catching toy, or a delicious sweet, and start pestering their dads or moms until they get what they want. So, what usually happens – as marketers know very well – is that the parent's initial NO is likely to turn into a YES, not out of generosity, but out of mere exhaustion. Simply put, they give up so their child will leave them alone.

Other parents are stricter, and their refusal is categorical. My father was one of them. He would say NO to many things: NO to pleasure, NO to the vacation, and NO to life as a whole. It was a NO to anything not related to school, work, or duty in general. Saying NO in these instances can be very detrimental to the self in the case of a person living on their own, or to the collective, in the case of a family or group of people. My rich-minded mother would also say NO to many things, but definitely not to life. Having always put her family first, she would still consider her job and housework priorities, but not the center of her universe. In this respect, Tony's NOs were definitely categorical. The only issue is that they were about the wrong stuff. In fact, denying oneself for the sake of profits, or work in general, can lead to a poorly lived life. It is a very poor strategy to aim towards accumulating money in the now, but to the detriment of life in the long run. For my part, I decided to use the best of both worlds. I took from my father his disciplined and categorical character, and from my mother, the ability to focus on satisfaction and self-fulfilment. I became both categorical and disciplined, but for things that really mattered. Why? To have the privilege and honor of fighting for a life that would be richly lived, which is infinitely more important that money and social statuses.

While it is dead easy to say YES, saying NO implies a level of risk. In fact, it takes courage to stand one's ground, and to be firm on one's initial decisions, whatever they are. You will agree that it takes a great deal of guts to be unavailable to one's superiors on your time off, especially if you have already made some plans. It takes even more determination to speak up when something wrong or unfair occurs. Unfortunately, everyone knows when unpleasant events happen, but very few are willing to step up and make their voices heard. By contrast, it is way faster to go for the easy road. That is, to bow one's heads, nodding in agreement all the time, still muttering under their breath, but without letting slip a word for fear of repercussions. In doing so, a long, peaceful career (and existence as a whole) is guaranteed, but to the detriment of never having your voice heard, not to mention your rights or personal needs.

Disagreeing takes lots of courage, particularly when it comes to injustice, or when someone is taking advantage of your kindness and availability. Like on the battlefield, it is much easier to fall back, rather than standing your ground. Likewise, in football, rugby, and other similar sports, losing ground is always easier and risk-free. It is when you want to gain ground that it becomes way more difficult. The same holds true for life. Carving out your own space (in the case of sports) or respect (in the case of work) takes guts. It implies not bowing your head, no matter what, especially when it looks patently unfair. The world is packed with all sorts of injustices for the simple fact that we don't fight for what we stand for. In habitually being silent, we indirectly accept whatever is given to us. Good and bad, ethical and unethical, all too often we let others decide for us, or worse, crush us!

The big problem lies exactly here: in the past, many grandparents (and Tony's family was no exception) used to teach their children (our parents) to always swallow bitter pills. And now, decades later, parents are roughly teaching their children to do the same. *Don't speak out. Obey what you are told. Always nod without question,* etc. There are exceptions to the rule, of course, but this is what I have noticed happening among my peers. Despite the ascent of new generations, the mindset and ideas remain mostly identical within families. *Don't complain. Accept what you get offered. Have a safe job. Earn enough. Retire happily.* While this could be a wise piece of advice in tough times, some have forgotten that we now live in a better-off era. We have more opportunities not just to study, but also to bring out the best in us. That said, you should aim high and make a point of raising your standards year by year. Don't forget that you are entitled to one life, and one only. So what's the point of not living it to the fullest now, and then having regrets in the future when it is too late?

The same holds true for colleagues' invitations or friends' favors. In an effort not to appear rude, we are inclined to be more available than we actually are – and all of this for fear of being excluded or getting labelled in a negative way. Not surprisingly, many teens do the most foolish things for the sake of this sense of belonging: getting drunk, taking up smoking, joining bullies, following idiotic trends, and so on.

Again, saying YES seems to be a guarantee against most problems. And not just that, it can enable us to feel part of something, or to simply get accepted by those we consider our friends. Some will help even when we might have our own things left to do. Some will give more than they can actually afford. While this can be admirable in terms of altruism, what is the actual price for such gestures? Don't forget that saying YES to something or someone implies taking your time, focus, and energy off something else. If you agree to help a colleague in need, or decide to work overtime, you will by default have less time for yourself and your family, not to mention your own projects and goals. This is when we need to learn to say NO in order to reclaim our own time and space. Money is refundable. Most things are returnable. Time is not! Once it is gone, it is gone. So, do your best to use it thoughtfully. You won't always be able to do so, I know, but being aware of this is already a starting point.

If you don't know where to begin, you can start by simply avoiding timewasters and opportunists. The former, as the word says, comprises all the undecided. Being insecure by nature, they have a habit of never taking a clear stance. They tend to always say, "Maybe," or, "We will see," or, "I don't know," and give all sorts of vague answers. This makes them waste their own time as well as yours. Since yours is too precious to go to waste, simply dismiss them by claiming you are too busy at the minute, or the like. The opportunists are even worse. Not only do they waste your time, but they try to rob it from you completely. Aware of the fact that you are a good-hearted, available person, they know they can always count on you for any personal favors. At work, for instance, if you are "yes person" to whom will the boss go anytime there is a shortage of staff? Exactly. You! As an opportunist is someone who just likes to receive, and rarely to give back, do yourself a favor and learn to stand your ground and reclaim your space. Just because you did a lot for them already, that does not mean they can use you forever. For the record, my rich-minded mother was an available person, too. As such, she taught me to be likewise. She did so because to her, friendship was all about mutual help. Unfortunately, in behaving like that, she came across many opportunists and scroungers. That's why I learned from her to be generous and kind, and from my father, to have an iron will, and say categorical NOs anytime someone was pushing my generosity too far. Since then, no one ever stepped on my toes, nor my time or space again.

Be a rich-minded person (and parent) yourself:

Being too available has both ups and downs. On the one hand, it makes you appear to be the nicest person in the room, the one to always turn to anytime one needs a favor. On the other hand, you will have less time, focus, and energy left for your personal things. Again, nothing is free in this world; the same goes for your time. Generations go by, but in many cases, the mindset remains unchanged. *Don't argue. Do what you are told, even when it seems wrong. Stay away from trouble. Don't complain,* and so on. This means bowing your head even when the boss is wrong, and staying silent even when you are dead right. As nothing is free, if you accept injustices, you are also giving out the message that people can do whatever they want with you and your time. If you were taught this by poor-minded parents or grandparents, think again about the outcome. You are not to be taken for granted, nor should your time or availability. Learn to draw the line at what you consider unacceptable. That way, you will not only be admired for your availability, but also respected for your iron will.

THE COURAGE TO PERSIST

*"If my mind can conceive it, and my heart
can believe it, then I can achieve it."*
—**Muhammad Ali, world-renowned
heavyweight boxing champion, activist**

As humans, we are made up of emotions. We love to dream and castle-build about all the things we would like to do, achieve and enjoy. This is particularly recurrent when December approaches, and we make all sorts of plans and goals to ensure a better year ahead. But then what happens? The New Year finally arrives, but we are not ready to deal with what was initially in our minds. This is when excuses take their toll and we put off to an indefinite time what we have initially promised to do.

It is the case that only a tiny percentage stick to the initial plans and reach completion. Some will either toe-dip, giving up shortly afterwards, while others won't even kick off, making up all sorts of explanations as to why they can't do it at the moment.

If you want to distinguish yourself from the masses – that is, to get started and bring whatever is in your mind to completion – you need to develop a burning desire for it. You can't just half-heartedly try; you must be serious and resolute about what's in your mind. If you develop such a habit, you will go places.

By the time I started university, I had learned from Mary that *success* is all about determination and persistence, not certificates, diplomas, and the like. An iron will is necessary to play the game and take on all the necessary corrections as you go. Despite knowing this, I enrolled in university more as a life experience than anything. Yet, deep down I knew that my behavior would be the thing that made a difference in the end; not my degree or grades, but my daily actions, along with my willingness to remain open and flexible in the face of adversities.

One of the secrets to success is to actually get started, whether you are ready or not. Second, being curious and willing to learn from those who are more knowledgeable than you. They will bring you closer to achieving your goals. For those who are willing and humble enough to pick up something every day and from the right people, chances are they will succeed more often than those who stop learning after school. Last, experimenting on yourself with what works and what doesn't, and making prompt corrections along the way, will steer you in the right direction.

Where there are no risks to be taken, there are no deeds to achieve either.

As Vincent Van Gogh, the famous artist, put it, "Normality is a paved road: it's comfortable to walk on, but no flowers grow on it."[13]

Leading an ordinary life is the quickest way to safety and tranquillity, but it stops there. As in Van Gogh's words, no opportunities are likely to knock on the door of those who decide to play it safe all the time. Unconsciously or not, those who habitually bow their heads and give up easily are in for a very average life.

We may have gaps in this field and voids in that area, but this is just a temporary condition due to our lack of preparation or inexperience. Sadly, the vast majority mistakenly believe that limitations are permanent. Our limiting beliefs tend to block us in whatever we do. How? By doubting ourselves and taking a step back (rather than forward) when opportunities arise. Tony had built up many limiting beliefs over the years. It came as no surprise, then, that he led an average life made up of working hard, saving up, with little or no stimulations. He may have had quite a healthy bank account in his sixties, but at the price of almost zero emotions.

By the time I finished high school, and after my parents' divorce, I knew whom to listen to, and whom to ignore. Mary wisely taught me that no amount of money can be traded for happiness and self-fulfilment. Instead, the best way I could use money was on self-education. Investing in myself in a productive, self-rewarding way became very valuable. Courses, books, or travelling not as a tourist, all would widen my horizons, and break down those limiting beliefs that people naturally build up inside themselves due to eternal sameness.

The best evidence was that of not thinking that the world is limited to our own reality. The same holds true for opportunities. If something doesn't work, it is not the end of the world. If you failed, perhaps you were not meant for it. Instead of getting depressed, stand up and look around yourself. There might be something better just around the corner.

In addition, when facing adversities, which are so typical when leaving the comfort zone and exploring new, uncharted territories, how would you behave? Would you stand firm, or would you rather tremble and simply back off? This question was not asked randomly. If you are used to comforts, you will almost surely feel uneasy when facing problems, bad surprises, and all manner of unexpected events. By contrast, if you are someone who had been pushed to the limit on numberless occasions, you will feel at ease in any given circumstances:

When you master yourself, you master your life.

It is when you have this sort of courage and resilience that you are more likely to persist in the presence of the ups and downs so typical of everyday life.

Speaking of ups and downs, the courage to persist made all the difference to me. Sure, we also need some luck from time to time, but other than that, it is our perseverance that does the trick. Those who bail out easily and quickly are the real losers. It is such a shame that many poor-minded parents teach their children to give up quickly and repeatedly, not realizing that, in doing so, they are unconsciously teaching them to *lose*. Conversely, those who have rich-minded parents learn first in theory, and then in practice, how critical being perseverant is. Walt Disney is a case in point. He faced bankruptcy, mental breakdowns, and he even lost the copyright over his very first creation, *Oswald the Lucky Rabbit*®. Despite all this, Disney got up, learned a lesson, and his perseverance made him keep going. He could have stayed down, and complained about how unfair life is and how mean some people can be. Yet, no! He decided to move on, knowing he still had something for himself…his *imagination*. Bear in mind, the world is full of talented people, but talent alone does not do the trick. The magic happens when you combine your talent – whatever it is – with a strong determination to turn your ideas into reality and give them a tangible form. Walt Disney did not come from a wealthy family, nor had he money to spare. He merely blended talent and perseverance. After that, finding someone to finance his projects was not a big deal. In my view:

> **When you have a great idea,**
> **and are passionate about it,**
> **the "how" always develops on the way.**

People buy certainty. An investor is more likely to back someone whose heart and tears went into something, rather than someone who may be very talented, but their heart is not in it. When your heart is into something, you will know it. People around you will perceive it, too. It is when you don't have passing thoughts that you will prove how serious and determined you are. Similarly, it is when you don't change your mind very often that you show how serious you are about one single thing instead of many.

This is reason enough to consider single-tasking, rather than multi-tasking. In the former, you are single-minded with what's on your plate, and you are most likely to give it one hundred percent. By contrast, when you multi-task, very rarely will you give blood, sweat and tears for each task. Too focused on many things at the same time, you split your focus, attention, and effort to the point that giving one hundred percent is virtually impossible:

> **Talent is good, but without**
> **a good dose of perseverance,**
> **nothing will come out of the hat.**

Like with plants, you may have the best soil in town, but if you don't nurture your seeds and shoots constantly with water and care, nothing special will come of them. The same holds true for personal goals. If you don't single-handedly dedicate yourself to them, a wish will remain what it is – a mere *wish*. The same goes for any good thoughts. They will never reach a tangible form if you don't believe in yourself first.

If I have a satisfactory job in foreign languages now, and I am passionate about what I do daily, it is entirely thanks to Mary. She thought me to THINK BIG, RISK BIG, and, more importantly, BELIEVE IN MYSELF. Those were the ingredients to living life to the fullest, and to being happy as a whole.

Waking up motivated and going to bed satisfied are fundamental to a fulfilling life. Also, I think it is a birthright to feel happy within, rather than just trying to keep afloat. The good news is, if an ordinary person like me did it, so can you. But, and this is a big BUT: are you willing to pay the price that success usually demands? That is, are you willing to work hard even on the weekends, be disciplined, and keep yourself going despite naysayers all around you?

Whether parents know it or not, they play a key role in all this. They provide input to their children's future choices. Be it college, university, or even going straight to work after school, moms and dads are the prime educators when it comes to valuable advice. As such, they should take their own upbringing to heart, and sew their little minds with rich thoughts and optimism, rather than bringing up their children to play it safe, and passing on the idea that the world is limited, cruel, and scarce of opportunities. If they do the latter, they are unconsciously sabotaging their boys and girls by clipping their wings, the same wings that would let them fly high, very high, indeed. Don't be the killer of your children's dreams.

Be a rich-minded person (and parent) yourself:

Getting started is always easy. Persisting against adversities is a totally different story. If your idea is very good, but have a weak will in the motivational side of things, you won't reap that many fruits at the end of the day. This is why it is important to know exactly what you want and clarify your priorities. Once you know this, tailor a plan to guide you through it, especially when you happen to feel lost or confused. This is also the reason why single-tasking is preferable to multi-tasking. When your focus is on one objective only, your attention is one hundred percent on it; you are more likely to give all you've got, and perform brilliantly as a result. By contrast, when you have many things on the plate, you may spread yourself so thinly to the point of doing everything averagely. Be clear on what you want. Choose one or two tasks only, and develop a plan to stick with it all the way through. Magic happens to the perseverant; very little magic happens to the toe-dipper. As a rich-minded person by now, you know which one to choose.

CONCLUSION

We went through a number of topics regarding the main differences between a rich-minded parent versus a poor-minded one. Persistence, limitations, grades, respect, family, and many other topics were put in place for one single purpose: to make you *reflect*. Now, suppose you are a parent yourself (now or anytime soon), what kind of parent would you be? Someone like Mary or Tony? How would you behave with your little ones in day-to-day challenges? And, more importantly, regardless of how you were brought up in your heyday, as a parent, what would you teach your own sons or daughters now? Would you simply "copy and paste" the teachings from your own old buddies or would you rather create your own?

Almost surely, you will have sympathized with Mary throughout the book, but be honest with yourself and answer these questions: if you were to go through the same circumstances as Mary did, would you still do, advise, and behave as she did? Would you really stand firm with your ideas, arguing with your spouse, grandparents, or relatives, even if that would mean putting your marriage on the line?

Being raised by parents in a conservative way, Tony was more of a traditional type. To him, guarantees, saving up, settling for less, and living only after retirement were all uncompromisable principles. It was not his fault if he was brought up in an old-school, post-war way. However, it was he who was at fault for wanting to pass the same teachings on to me without any personal touch. By contrast, Mary made a point of breaking the parental cycle. She also had old-school parents and a behind-the-times upbringing. What made her different from Tony was her willingness to opt for flexibility of thought and freedom of action. She would prioritize quality moments and well-being, even if that would somewhat endanger safety and economic security.

As you will have noticed by now, this book was a direct example of two parents: one who was in favor of my growth, the other (even if unconsciously) not. One of the takeaways of this book is to make both current and would-be parents aware of how easily they can lift their children up, as well as take them down with their thoughts and teachings. That said, be extra careful as to what you decide to plant into young minds. You will be aware that no one wins the game by playing on the defensive. Make sure to teach your children to habitually play on the attack, because only by moving forward is victory likely to occur.

By the same token, poor thoughts, followed up by weak action, will never bring about rich fruit. Instead, when you bravely move forward and act, that's when miracles are more likely to occur – not with the familiar toe-dipping we are so used to putting into place. As it all starts at a tender age, be mindful of what you transmit to your children, as any teachings you pass on can make a world of difference to them and their future.

My objective is to forge more rich-minded parents out there. In doing so, more rich-minded children will be living more fulfilled lives in the future. Since children cannot be self-taught in terms of upbringing, be thoughtful of what you sew into your children's minds. As they cannot think critically, make sure it is mainly richness (not poverty) in thoughts that they soak up from you. Sadly, many parents simply "park" their children at the schoolyard or with their grandparents, thinking that these others will look after them in all senses. This couldn't be more wrong, as it is your job as parents to educate children, raise them properly, teach them what's right and wrong, and how to live a great life.

Be the parent you wish you had.

Here comes the best bit. In case you haven't had very nice parents, what better chance of being the parent you wish you had? The previous chapters have shown how a poor-minded parent moves and behaves versus a rich-minded one. That being said, are you more like Mary or Tony in day-to-day circumstances?

To help you out in this, below is a straightforward exercise, the aim of which is to highlight the differences between the parents you had and the one you want to be yourself. It looks at how you were educated versus how you intend to raise your loved ones now (or anytime soon).

How was I raised in my childhood?

_____

_____

_____

_____

_____

What were the teachings I was taught to live by?

_____

_____

_____

_____

_____

_____

_____

If I were (or am already) a parent myself, how would I behave in order to be a better parent? Or better, the parent I wish I had?

_____

_____

_____

_____

_____

_____

_____

_____

What steps can I take to be a rich-minded parent?

_____

_____

_____

_____

_____

_____

_____

This simple exercise can help you gain more clarity as a parent, and help you make better decisions for your children. In case you feel stuck, have questions, or don't know how to go ahead with any of the above questions, you are not alone. At any time, you are warmly invited to join the Facebook community, *The Greatest Version of Yourself,* a place to get in touch with the author, as well as other like-minded people. It is a platform created to share ideas and inspire one another to make this a better world.

Many know that everything starts out as a thought or an idea, but only a few are aware that:

*It is what we decide to do with that thought
or idea that may change the world we live in.
Be a rich-minded person (and parent) yourself.*

References

1. Ruiz, D. M. (1997). *The Four Agreements.* San Rafael, CA. Amber-Allen Publishing. 5.

2. Sharma, R. R. (1997) *The Man who Sold his Ferrari: A fable about fulfilling your dreams and reaching your destiny.* New York, NY. Harper Collins. 194.

3. Knight, T. A. (nd) https://www.goodreads.com/author/quotes/5324316. Thomas. A. Knight

4. Peale, N. V. (2005/1956). *The Power of Positive Thinking.* Quality Paperback Book Club. http://www.qpbc.com/ 228.

5. Sharma, R. R. op cit., 199.

6. Brown, L. (nd) https://www.brainyquotes.com/citation/quotes/les brown 370156

7. Coelho, P. (1993/1988). *The Alchemist.* New York. Harper Collins Publishers, Inc. 16.

8. Covey, S. (2004/1989) *The 7 Habits of Highly Effective People: Restoring the character ethic.* New York. Simon & Schuster. 346.

9. Ghandi, M. (nd) https://www.brainyquotes/quotes/mahatma ghandi 109075

10. Einstein, A. (1987). *The Collected Papers of Albert Einstein.* Princeton, NJ. Princeton University Press. 55.

11. Peale, N. V. op cit., 102.

12. Johnson, D. (2021). *"The Rock" Great notebook of Dwayne Johnson.* Patrickox Books. eBook.

13. Van Gogh, V. (nd). quotefancy.com/vincent-van-gogh-quotes

About Kharis Publishing:

Kharis Publishing, an imprint of Kharis Media LLC, is a leading Christian and inspirational book publisher based in Aurora, Chicago metropolitan area, Illinois. Kharis' dual mission is to give voice to under-represented writers (including women and first-time authors) and equip orphans in developing countries with literacy tools. That is why, for each book sold, the publisher channels some of the proceeds into providing books and computers for orphanages in developing countries so that these kids may learn to read, dream, and grow. For a limited time, Kharis Publishing is accepting unsolicited queries for nonfiction (Christian, self-help, memoirs, business, health and wellness) from qualified leaders, professionals, pastors, and ministers. Learn more at: https://kharispublishing.com/